HIDDEN POWER

How to Unleash the Power
of Your Subconscious Mind

HIDDEN POWER

How to Unleash the Power of Your Subconscious Mind

James K. Van Fleet

PRENTICE HALL

Library of Congress Cataloging-in-Publication Data

Van Fleet, James K.
    Hidden power.
    Includes index.
    ISBN 0-13-386897-4—ISBN 0-13-386889-3 (pbk.)
    1. Success.   2. Subconsciousness.   I. Title.
    BJ1611.2.V36   1987   87-25932
    1588'.1   CIP

Printed in the United States of America

34

ISBN 0-13-386897-4   ISBN 0-13-386889-3 (PBK)

PRENTICE HALL
Paramus, NJ 07652

On the World Wide Web at http://www.phdirect.com

This book is dedicated to those people who have made my life well worthwhile.

First, my wife, Belva LaVonne Van Fleet, who has been the light of my life for more than 45 years.

Next, to my children whom I also consider to be my friends,

Robert James Van Fleet

Teresa Lynne Van Fleet

Lawrence Lee Van Fleet

Third, to those people who have joined my children and brought joy into their lives,

G. Arch Spain

Joanie Patterson Cook

Suzanne Colleen Welch

Last, to my grandchildren who have brought much joy and happiness to me,

Adam Lucas Spain

Joel Van Spain

Kelley Michelle Cook

Christina Lynne Van Fleet

Dara Nicole Van Fleet

Jessica Marie Van Fleet

Leah Brooke Van Fleet

Other Books by the Author

*A Doctor's Proven New Way to Conquer Rheumatism and
Arthritis*
Lifetime Conversation Guide
The Magic of Catalytic Health Vitalizers
Power with People
25 Steps to Power and Mastery over People
*The 22 Biggest Mistakes Managers Make and How to
Correct Them*
How to Use the Dynamics of Motivation
How to Put Yourself Across with People
Extraordinary Healing Secrets from a Doctor's Private Files
Doctor Van Fleet's Amazing New "Non-Glue-Food" Diet
Guide to Managing People
Van Fleet's Master Guide for Managers
Miracle People Power

What This Book Will Do for You

This book, *Hidden Power: How to Unleash the Power of Your Subconscious Mind*, is about a discovery I made that has brought me a more than satisfactory share of the good things in life. I know that when you make the same discovery I did, then you, too, will gain a greater abundance of whatever it is that you most deeply desire.

For example, I know you will be able to gain your goals of love and respect from others as well as fame, fortune, power, and vibrant good health. Nor will you have to use the trial-and-error methods that I used, for I have outlined the route for you to follow in this book, so you can quickly and easily reach your desired goals.

Let me now just briefly tell you what this book is all about and exactly what it can do for you. You see, within every human being is an infinite, unlimited, and powerful force that works even better than the most sophisticated modern computer you could ever imagine. That infinite, unlimited, and powerful force in every person is the *subconscious mind.*

But do not think for one moment that you can compare your subconscious mind with a manmade computer, for you cannot. The difference between the two is far too great. The manmade computer does not exist, and never will, that can come anywhere near the powerful capabilities of your subconscious mind.

Unfortunately, most people go through life without ever realizing that this tremendously powerful subconscious mind even exists, let alone understanding how to use it properly to get whatever they want. Only a small percentage discovers the subconscious mind, understands it, and then learns how to use its hidden power to achieve complete success in whatever they set out to do.

Helping you develop your ability, not only to contact, but also to communicate with your subconscious mind so you can use its unlimited and infinite power to become successful in everything you do is my specific purpose in writing this book. And you can become successful in all your endeavors when you understand exactly what the subconscious mind is and how you can use its hidden power to make it work for your own benefit.

For example, let me tell you about just a few of the good things that can be yours when you know how to use your subconscious mind properly to get what you want out of life. These few examples do not constitute a complete list of all the many benefits that can be yours by any means. They are only a small sampling of all the good things that can be yours.

1. When you know how to use the hidden power of your subconscious mind properly, you can become materially successful and rich beyond your wildest dreams. Your subconscious mind can activate your imagination and inspire you with new thoughts and fresh ideas that will be highly profitable and bring you unlimited material success. You can use the power of your subconscious mind to gain the financial prosperity that will give you the freedom to be whatever you want to be, do whatever you want to do, and go wherever and whenever your heart desires.

2. You can use your subconscious mind to rid yourself of frustration, anger, and resentment. Its hidden power will help you solve your most pressing problems and lead you to the right decisions. You can also use the power of your subconscious mind to free yourself from fear, anxiety, and worry forever as well as to deactivate and defuse your failure attitudes and ideas and replace them with positive and successful ones.

3. When you use the hidden power of your subconscious mind properly, you will be able to enjoy abundant and radiant health. Just getting rid of frustration, anger, and resentment will improve your health tremendously. You'll bubble over with vitality, energy, and enthusiasm for living. Life will truly become worthwhile for each day will be filled to the brim with the sheer joy of being alive.

4. Have you ever felt out of place in life as if you were a useless fifth wheel? You can use your subconscious mind to help you find your true place and to help keep you in it, too. It will help you determine what you are best fitted to do so you can use your innate abilities to the maximum. Through its hidden power, you'll be able to find the right

job so you can be happy in what you do for a living. You'll be able to go to work each day with a happy smile and a joyous heart instead of a sour attitude and a frown.

Your subconscious mind is lying there dormant within you just waiting for you to use it. It is a source of energy stronger than electricity, more powerful than high explosive. Your subconscious mind is unlimited, infinite, and inexhaustible. It never rests, for it keeps right on working for you even when you are asleep. You need only to activate it and put its power to work in your life so that all those marvelous benefits I've told you about can be yours.

James K. Van Fleet

Contents

How You Can Use the Hidden Power of Your Subconscious Mind to Work Literal Miracles for You

YOUR DUAL MIND

You have two minds, the conscious one and the subconscious one. Your conscious mind uses logic, deduction, and reason to reach its conclusions and to make its decisions. Your choices in life, your decisions as to what you will or will not do are made by your conscious mind, not by your subconscious mind. However, when you learn how to use your subconscious mind properly, you will find that the choices and decisions made by your conscious mind will be guided and influenced by the information received from your subconscious mind.

Your subconscious mind does not think or act on its own volition or its own initiative. *Its primary purpose is to achieve the goals that have been given to it by your conscious mind.*

If you do not give your subconscious mind any goals to reach or problems to solve, it will never work for you. But if you do give it

1

specific goals and concrete objectives to attain—for example: a new house, an expensive car, a better job, and so on—it will go all-out to achieve them for you.

I will discuss these functions of the conscious and subconscious minds in greater detail later on in this chapter, but for now, I want to tell you. . . . .

How Your Subconscious Mind Works Like a Computer

My own research and study of anatomy, physiology, biology, and applied psychology for more than 40 years have led me to realize that the subconscious mind works much like a manmade computer. Its functions and actions are directed by the conscious mind.

The subconscious mind is a sophisticated electronic goal-seeking mechanism that functions much like any manmade computer, but it is much more complex and intricate than the most complicated computer ever conceived by man.

As one eminent scientist has said, "The subconscious mind works like a computer, but there is no computer like the subconscious mind." This gentleman went on to say that at no time in the foreseeable future would science be able to construct a computer anywhere near comparable to the subconscious mind.

Even if a computer could be built that would be as sophisticated, as complex, and as intricate as the subconscious mind, it would still need a human being's conscious mind to operate it. A manmade computer does not have a built-in conscious mind to direct its actions as your subconscious mind has. Nor can a manmade computer pose original problems to itself. It has no imagination and cannot set its own goals. Nor does it have emotions to help it make the correct moral decisions. A manmade computer can work only on the data supplied to it from the outside by its human operator.

Although the subconscious mind operates less rapidly and less accurately in some respects than a manmade computer does, simply because it is human and not a machine and therefore subject to all the emotions of the conscious mind, even the most advanced computer is left far behind when it is compared with the subconscious mind's staggering capacity to accomplish the unbelievably difficult tasks that are assigned to it to solve. After all, the computer was born in the mind of man, not the other way around.

How Your Subconscious Mind Works for You

Although this entire book will show you how to use the hidden power of your subconscious mind to become successful in everything you do, I want to use this small section here to give you some very basic and fundamental facts about how your subconscious mind works to attain the goals you've given to it.

Let me do this by giving you an extremely simple example: that of feeding yourself. You are able to accomplish this goal of eating because of a habit pattern that has been programmed into your subconscious mind a countless number of times. You do not have to use your conscious mind to tell your subconscious mind to move the fork from your plate to your mouth.

Nor do you have to think about which muscles you should contract to accomplish this goal of eating. Your subconscious mind has been programmed by previous experience to perform the proper movements to move the food from the plate to your mouth without any action whatever on the part of your conscious mind. Nor do you need to use your eyes to guide the fork to your mouth. The movements have all become entirely automatic.

But this is not true with a baby learning to eat by itself. The infant smears food all over its face in an attempt to hit its mouth. After what seems like an eternity to impatient parents, the child does learn to feed itself without making an absolute mess of it.

My purpose in giving you this simple example is to show you that *once a correct or successful response has been established in your subconscious mind that allows it to attain the specific goal you've given it with your conscious mind, that procedure is then stored and remembered for future use.*

Your subconscious mind repeats this successful response on future trials, no matter what they are—eating, riding a bicycle, driving a car, playing golf, tennis, catching a ball, playing a piano, guitar, whatever. It has learned to respond properly because that is what your conscious mind has directed it to do. Your subconscious mind remembers its successes, discards its failures, and repeats the successful actions as a matter of habit without any further thought or direction from your conscious mind.

In fact, certain habit patterns are so deeply ingrained in your subconscious mind that the goals given to it by your conscious mind can be easily accomplished in the dark or when your eyes are closed. No light is needed to touch your nose, scratch your ear, rub your eye, or put food in your mouth. You can do all these things in the dark just as a blind person can do them, for your subconscious mind remembers exactly where each part of your body is.

How Athletes Use the Subconscious Mind to Succeed in Sports

Let me give you another example of how your subconscious mind will accomplish your goals automatically for you with very little thought or direction from your conscious mind. Take a professional baseball player; for instance, an outfielder.

At the crack of the bat on the ball, the fielder is off and running. Without even thinking about it with his conscious mind, because of past experience, that outfielder's subconscious mind has taken over. It has taken into consideration the direction of the ball, its speed, the velocity and direction of the wind, and how fast that player must run to be at the exact spot necessary to catch the ball.

If you are a baseball fan, you've seen this happen time after time. The outfielder makes it look easy, all because the stored information in his subconscious mind makes it so. This same concept or principle applies to any sport: tennis, golf, bowling, whatever. The top professionals have learned to relax and let their subconscious minds do all the work for them.

Even if your ball playing consists of no more than playing catch in the backyard with your son, I know you don't have to look at your glove to catch the ball, even if it's away over your head where you cannot see it. You catch it instinctively because your subconscious mind tells you exactly where to hold your glove because of its past experience in helping you catch a ball.

Your Subconscious Mind Makes No Moral Judgments

Your subconscious mind is completely impersonal. It is not capable of making moral judgements or determining the difference between right and wrong, good or evil. That is the sole responsibility of your conscious mind.

Your subconscious mind will work automatically and impersonally to achieve the goals you have set for it, no matter what they are, good or evil, right or wrong, moral or immoral. If you will remember, that is the primary purpose and responsibility of your subconscious mind: to achieve the goals and objectives that have been given to it by your conscious mind.

If you have ever wondered why or how some dishonest people can be so successful, this is the reason. Their subconscious minds have achieved the goals their conscious minds have set for them, even though those goals are evil, immoral, or illegal. By the same token, you've seen some good and honest people fail miserably. Why? Because they failed to give their subconscious minds the proper goals to reach.

As you can see from this, it matters not to your subconscious mind what its goals are. If you program it for success, you will be successful. If you program it for failure, you will fail.

The choice is entirely up to you. If you give your subconscious mind success goals, it will function as a success mechanism for you. If you offer it failure goals or negative objectives to reach, it will function as a failure mechanism for you. In this respect, you can see that your subconscious mind works exactly like a manmade computer in that *output always equals input*, a point I will discuss with you in complete detail in Chapter 4.

How Your Conscious Mind Works

Your conscious mind is that part of your brain that enables you to know, to think, and to act effectively. Your conscious mind uses logic, deduction, and reasoning to reach its conclusions and make its decisions. Your choices, your decisions as to what you will or will not do are made by your conscious mind, not by your subconscious mind.

It is your conscious mind that takes cognizance of the objective world around you. Its method of observing its environment is to use your five physical senses: sight, smell, sound, touch, taste. You gain knowledge through these five senses. Your conscious mind learns through observation, experience, and education. Perhaps the greatest function of your conscious mind is that of using logic, deduction, and reason. This marks one of the greatest differences between man and animal.

When you say, "I see . . . I hear . . . I smell, taste, or touch," it is your conscious mind saying these things. Your conscious mind also controls all your voluntary muscles; your subconscious mind controls all your involuntary muscles through the spinal cord and autonomic nervous system.

It is only through your conscious mind that you can contact your subconscious mind. It is to your conscious mind that your subconscious mind looks for instructions. Without these instructions from your conscious mind, your subconscious mind can do nothing for you, for it has no goals to reach.

One of the most important duties of your conscious mind is to tell your subconscious mind what you want and then to believe with all your heart that you will receive what you have asked for. You must shut the door of your conscious mind on every thought or suggestion of worry or fear of failure. Once you gain the ability to do this, absolutely nothing is impossible for you to achieve.

But if you program your subconscious mind improperly with fear, worry, and anxiety, it will bring those fears into reality for you. As Job said, "For the thing which I greatly feared is come upon me, and that which I was afraid of is come unto me" (Job 3:25). If you have fears, they can come true for you just as they did for Job several thousand years ago.

Understanding the Relationship Between the Conscious and Subconscious Minds

To help you better understand the relationship between the conscious and subconscious minds and how they work together in harmony with each other, let me give you this example:

Your conscious mind is like the captain of a ship. That ship's captain is in complete control. He directs all the activities of his ship. He issues orders to the crew in the engine room who controls the intricate and complicated machinery that runs the ship. If the captain issued improper or faulty orders to his crew, the ship could end up sinking in a storm or being torn to pieces on a rocky coast. The members of his crew can only follow orders; they cannot see where the ship is actually going.

The ship's captain is the lord and master of all that he surveys, more so perhaps than any other person in a leadership position in this world. No one in the crew dares dispute his orders. Everyone obeys his commands and carries out his instructions to the letter. Another comparable person in such a leadership position would be the captain and chief pilot of an airplane.

This is exactly how your conscious mind directs your subconscious mind to do its work. Just as the captain of a ship is its master, so is your conscious mind the master of your subconscious mind. Your subconscious mind accepts its orders from your conscious mind, be they positive or negative, right or wrong, and carries them out for you without question. That is why it is so important that you give your subconscious mind only positive goals to reach.

Your subconscious mind does not use logic or reason or moral judgment to perform its tasks or carry out its responsibilities. It takes the thoughts you send to it and works them out to their proper conclusions. If you send it thoughts of health and strength, it will bring health and strength to your body. But if you let suggestions of disease or fear of sickness penetrate through to your subconscious mind, either through your own thoughts or the *talk of those around you*, then you can easily become sick yourself.

Let me give you another quick example of how you can give your subconscious mind improper orders or negative suggestions that will cause you to fail. For instance, if your conscious mind tells your subconscious mind that you are poor and can never afford a big house or a new car, you can be assured that you will never have either of them, or anything else worthwhile, for that matter, for you have given your subconscious mind the wrong goals to reach. I will discuss how you can give your subconscious mind the right goals and the proper objectives in complete detail in Chapter 7.

OTHER FUNCTIONS OF YOUR SUBCONSCIOUS MIND

Although I will cover most of these points at greater length in individual chapters, I want to give you here a sort of summary or synopsis of the various functions of your subconscious mind so I can show you, not only how to use it to attain success in whatever you choose to do, but also, what the rest of this book is all about.

I would ask that for better understanding of your conscious and subconscious minds, you keep one thought fixed firmly in mind, not only as you read this chapter but also, as you read every chapter in the rest of this book. I have already mentioned this point twice before, but it cannot be repeated too often for it is so important for you to remember.

And that point is, of course, that *the primary purpose of your subconscious mind is to achieve the goals and objectives that have been given to it by your conscious mind.* If you will remember this, everything else will fall into place naturally of its own accord. Your questions will be answered almost automatically even before you ask them.

I will not cover in any depth the various functions of your body that are controlled by the involuntary nervous system, such as metabolism, digestion, breathing, and cardiovascular activity. These functions are normally carried out without any outside interference or without any requirements for direction on the part of your conscious mind.

However, in Chapter 11, where I discuss how your health can be improved by giving the proper instructions to your subconscious mind, I will show you the methods you can use to get rid of arthritis and rheumatism, how even "incurable" cancer can be helped by the subconscious mind, how you can treat asthma, allergies, high blood pressure, constipation, and other common ailments. You will see how a change in attitude programmed into your subconscious mind by your conscious mind can cure emotionally induced illnesses.

I could not possibly cover all the physical problems that can be improved or cured when the proper directions are given to the subconscious mind. Had I done that, the chapter on health would have quickly become a book all by itself. I have, however, covered many of the common ailments that trouble most people. Not only that, you'll discover that no matter what your particular problem is, it can be helped if you use the methods I describe in Chapter 11 to program your subconscious mind for better health.

Your Subconscious Mind Acts as Your Brain's Memory Bank

Before I discuss the various other functions of your subconscious mind, I want to tell you how it acts as your memory bank. Then you can even better understand its many other functions.

Your subconscious mind never forgets anything. That is why it is so important that you program it with positive success ideas rather than negative failure ones.

As you will learn in the chapter on improving your health with the hidden power of the subconscious mind, one man cured his "incurable" arthritis by programming his subconscious mind with happy and joyous thoughts.

Another man with cancer was still living seven years after the doctors had given him only six months to live! He, too, had discovered how to program his subconscious mind with positive goals for better health.

From just these two examples alone you will learn how important it is to fill your subconscious mind with positive success ideas rather than negative failure ones.

Information that has been fed into your subconscious mind is kept stored in it forever, even though there are times when your conscious mind cannot seem to recall it. But even if your conscious mind may not be able to temporarily remember some name, some event, or some incident, that does not mean it has been forgotten. The information that is stored in your subconscious mind is never lost. It sometimes takes a bit more effort for your conscious mind to bring it up to the surface.

Under the proper conditions, when the conscious mind is put to rest and your subconscious mind is allowed to function at the Alpha rather than the Beta level, the incident that seems to be completely forgotten can then be recalled quite easily. I will discuss this with you at greater length in the next chapter.

How the Power of Your Subconscious Mind Can Help You Solve Problems and Make the Right Decisions

When you can't make up your mind, solve your problem, or reach a decision by logic, deduction, and reasoning, then it's time to turn things over to your subconscious mind so it can get the answer for you. In the next chapter, I'll give you examples of successful people who do that so you can see how to do it yourself. I'll also give you a problem-solving technique that you can use to help speed up the process so you can get your answers even faster.

Knowing how to solve problems and make the correct decisions will not only help you become successful and rich, but it will also help you in your social activities and relationships with people as well.

This problem-solving technique not only will show you how to use your conscious mind to solve your problems, but also shows how and when to turn those problems over to your subconscious mind to solve when your conscious mind just cannot seem to come up with the right answers for you.

How to Use the Hidden Power of Your Subconscious Mind to Deactivate and Defuse Your Failure Ideas

In Chapter 5, I'll show you how to deactivate and defuse your failure ideas with the proper programming of your subconscious mind so you can become successful in everything that you do. If you have thought of yourself as a failure, or allowed others to program your subconscious mind with negative ideas, you'll see how you can make a complete turnaround and become the successful and happy person you have the God-given right to be.

I have seen F students change into straight-A students when they were shown how to program their subconscious minds for success. I've also seen business failures and unsuccessful salespeople transformed into dynamos of energy and vitality by the same process.

You can do the same when you learn how to feed your subconscious mind with success ideas instead of failure ideas. As a man thinks, so will he become. The outer conditions of a person's life will always be in harmony with the inner state of both his conscious and subconscious minds.

How You Can Develop a Winning Attitude

You, too, can become a winner in everything you do when you know how to program your subconscious mind with winning attitudes. If you are not sure of how to do this, you can take a look at all those people in Chapter 6 who are successful, so you can discover what their winning characteristics are.

When you do, I know you'll find, just as I have, that winners have certain qualities that set them apart from the crowd. They believe in themselves and in their own abilities. Winners smile; they have learned that taking things too seriously or having a sour attitude causes them to become losers instead of winners.

Winners also live in the ever-present now. They do not worry about past mistakes or the possibility of future failures. As the old cliché goes, they believe sincerely that yesterday is a cancelled check, tomorrow is only a promissory note, but that today is cold, hard cash.

How You Can Use the Power of Your Subconscious Mind to Become Successful and Rich

When you learn how to listen for and then act on the guidance you receive from your subconscious mind, you can become successful in everything that you do. And when you become successful, then you can also become rich if that is your desire and your ambition.

In Chapter 8, I will show you how to use the fresh ideas and inspiration you get from your subconscious mind to gain riches and financial success in your chosen field, no matter what it might be.

How You Can Use the Hidden Resources of Your Subconscious Mind to Get Rid of Fear, Anxiety, and Worry Forever

In Chapter 9, I'll show you how to live in day-tight compartments so you can rid yourself of past guilt and future fears. You'll see how you can live happily and make fear, anxiety, and worry all things of the past by programming your subconscious mind properly. Hundreds of thousands of people in Alcoholics Anonymous have learned to live sober, productive lives by using many of these same principles and techniques, some of them unwittingly, but still successfully.

How You Can Get Rid of Undesirable Habits

Do you want to stop drinking or smoking, get rid of a rotten temper, improve your personality, get rid of an inferiority complex, learn to lose weight permanently? I'll show you in Chapter 10 that it is not your willpower that you need to solve these personal problems, but imagination.

You'll learn that when imagination and willpower are in conflict, imagination always wins. That's why it is best to use imagination to solve problems like these, not willpower as so many people think. I'll show you exactly how you can use your imagination instead of your willpower so you can get rid of these undesirable habits and get the results you want.

More Ways You Can Use the Hidden Power of Your Subconscious Mind to Your Own Advantage

Let me just briefly mention a few more of the ways you can use the hidden power of your subconscious mind to your own advantage. You can use it to improve your personal relationships with others, not only your own family—your spouse and your children—but also your friends, your neighbors, and your business associates.

You may not be a professional golfer, bowler, tennis player, or a musician, but I am sure you would like to improve your golf score, your bowling average, become a better tennis player or pianist than you already are. In the last chapter, I will show you how you can use the hidden power of your subconscious mind to develop your natural abilities to the maximum. And finally, in that same chapter, you will learn how to use enthusiasm and perseverance to the hilt to get the best results possible from your subconscious mind.

How You Can Achieve Serenity and Peace of Mind

When you are operating on inner guidance from your subconscious mind and you no longer have to guess about making the right decision or doing the right thing, you will gain a serenity and peace of mind that you cannot imagine possible until it actually happens to you. That time will come when you faithfully practice the principles and techniques that you will learn throughout this entire book.

Everything will seem to work out naturally for you the way it should without any extra effort or push on your part. Mistakes will become fewer and fewer. When that happens, you'll be able to relax and let your subconscious mind do all the hard work for you.

Life will take on a new zest and meaning. Instead of just existing or merely getting by, you can really start living a life forever free of anxiety, fear, and worry . . . a life that is filled with abundant joy and happiness.

This chapter represents only a partial preview of what the hidden power of your subconscious mind can do for you and the marvelous benefits that can be yours when you learn how to use it properly.

So without further delay, let us get right on into Chapter 2 where I'll show you how to take the first step, and that is: *How to Communicate with Your Subconscious Mind.*

How to Communicate with Your Subconscious Mind

2

You can communicate with your subconscious mind by feeding information into it just as you would do with a manmade computer. For instance, if something has been bothering you, and you haven't been able to come up with the right solution to your problem, then you should turn it over to your subconscious mind to solve for you.

Of course, you must allow time for your subconscious mind to absorb and assimilate all the information you've given to it about your problem. Then you simply wait for the right answer to come to you as it most certainly will if you are patient enough.

I must point out to you that you cannot force the answer. The more you try to force your subconscious mind, the more stubborn it will become. You must relax and allow it to work without pressure or outside interference from your conscious mind. For example, I'm sure you've had something like this happen to you before. You try hard to think of someone's name, but the harder you try, the more elusive that name becomes.

Finally, in disgust you give up the struggle, forget about it, sit back, relax, and think about something else entirely. And then, as if out of the blue, the name suddenly pops up in your conscious mind. That's the way your subconscious mind works for you. It cannot be forced. Nor does it work on the same schedule as your conscious mind. It works only on its own schedule and its own timetable. But the important point is that given the proper amount of time, it will always work.

The relationship between your conscious mind and your subconscious mind can be best illustrated for you by this simple example:

Suppose, for instance, your son has a broken toy. He brings it to you, confident that you can fix it for him. He tells you he has tried to fix it himself, but he cannot, and he wants you to help him.

So you take the broken toy and begin work on it. Now obviously you could do the repairs more quickly and easily if you were left alone to do so without any outside interference. But your son, instead of watching quietly or going off to play with something else, stands by offering you meaningless advice on how to do the job. Perhaps he even reaches in trying to help, but he only hinders your work. In the end, he may even grab his toy back from you, saying he can see you can't fix it after all. And so the broken toy never does get repaired.

This same thing can happen to you if you don't turn your problem over to your subconscious mind with complete confidence that it can do the job for you. The point is, you must learn to trust the creativity of your subconscious mind to do its work and not jam it by becoming anxious or concerned as to whether it will or will not work for you.

You cannot force your subconscious mind to do its job by exerting effort on the part of your conscious mind. This only inhibits and jams the automatic creative mechanism. You must relax and let your subconscious mind work for you rather than trying to force it to work by using willpower.

THE FANTASTIC BENEFITS YOU'LL GAIN WHEN YOU KNOW HOW TO COMMUNICATE WITH YOUR SUBCONSCIOUS MIND

1. Your subconscious mind will solve problems for you that seem completely insoluble to your conscious mind.

2. Fresh new ideas and original ways of doing things will come to you from your subconscious mind that you never dreamed of before.

3. You'll learn to operate successfully using hunches and intuition as your guidance in difficult situations.

4. You'll be more relaxed, confident, and at ease in your work, your social relationships, your entire life.

5. You'll be able to attain your goals of love and respect from others, fame, fortune, power, and vibrant good health when you learn to communicate with your subconscious mind and then follow the guidance it gives you.

The Techniques You Can Use to Gain These Benefits

How you can use your conscious mind to solve problems

Not every problem you encounter has to be turned over to your subconscious mind to solve. Many problems can be handled by your conscious mind simply by using the information and past experiences that are recorded and stored in the memory banks of your subconscious mind. So first let me give you a concise six-step problem-solving technique you can use to get the answer from your conscious mind.

1. *Identify Your Exact Problem.* Determine exactly what your problem is and precisely how it's causing you trouble.

2. *Determine the Exact Cause of Your Problem.* You will want to know why and how your problem arose so you can correct the cause, not just treat its symptoms. So dig up all the facts that bear on your problem. The more you know about its cause, the better the position you'll be in to solve it.

3. *Determine All the Possible Solutions.* After you have found the basic cause of your problem, then consider all the possible solutions for it. Don't rule out a solution on first examination. Even if it later proves to be unusable, a tentative solution may contain ideas of value for the future. The more possible solutions you consider, the better your final one is likely to be.

4. *Evaluate the Possible Solutions.* When you've gathered together all the possible solutions, then compare one with the other. Don't let your personal preferences or prejudices influence you when you're evaluating suggestions from others. For instance, don't reject Brown's idea because he has bad breath or Smith's suggestion because he's such a sloppy dresser. Remember, too, if you jump to conclusions, you can often create a more serious problem than the one you're trying to solve.

5. *Pick the Best Solution with Your Conscious Mind.* A point well worth mentioning here, for it is often overlooked—even by the most experienced people in problem-solving or decision-making—is that your solution can be a combination of two or more of the possible solutions you've considered. For instance, you might take part of Black's suggestion, part of White's, and come up with a "Gray" solution that will solve the problem perfectly for you.

6a. *Put Your Solution into Effect—Take the Necessary Action.* This is the last step in the problem-solving process that is used by your conscious mind. It is often the biggest obstacle of all because of fear. But don't waver with indecision now. The hard work is over. If you are sure your solution is correct, step out with confidence and put it into effect; take the necessary action to solve your problem.

In some cases, this six-step problem-solving technique I've just given you is all you'll need to use. In other words, you'll be able to solve your problem with your conscious thinking mind, even though you will be using the experiences and previously recorded information that you have stored in your subconscious mind.

How your subconscious mind can solve your problems for you

Now let's say you've taken the first five steps in the problem-solving technique. You've identified your exact problem . . . you've determined its specific cause . . . you've figured out all the possible solutions . . . you've evaluated all the possible solutions . . . you may even have tentatively picked the best solution with your conscious thinking mind.

However, you are still hesitant to take the sixth step—that is, putting your solution into effect—for one of several reasons. Perhaps you can't make up your mind between two possible solutions. Perhaps you want to get confirmation on your tentative decision. Or maybe you don't have the slightest idea of what to do about your problem.

If any of these situations do exist, then you are in no position to put your solution into effect or take the necessary action as I showed you how to do in Step 6a of the problem-solving techniques. For you, *a completely different Step 6* is in order and here is what it is:

6b. *Turn Everything Over to Your Subconscious Mind* to solve your problem for you. Then relax and forget all about it. The right answer to your problem will be given to you as a hunch or a flash of intuition or inspiration.

Will this method work? It most certainly will. The chief of research at a large and well-known electrical manufacturing corporation told me that nearly all the discoveries in their research laboratories come as hunches or flashes of inspiration during a period of complete relaxation after a session of intensive thinking, brainstorming, and fact-gathering.

When the famous and prolific inventor, Thomas A. Edison, was baffled by some problem, he would cast it out of his conscious mind, turn everything over to his subconscious mind, lie down, take a short nap, and, then, more often than not, awake with the answer he needed to solve his problem.

It is important that you have complete confidence in the hidden power of your subconscious mind to do the job for you. Not only should you tell your subconscious mind what you want, but also, *exactly what you expect from it.* However, do not tell it *how* to solve your problem for you. You must leave that up to your subconscious mind to do. If you will simply relax and not interfere, it will do the required work for you.

7. *When You Receive the Answer from Your Subconscious Mind, Act Upon the Instructions You Receive.* When you get the answer to the problem from your subconscious mind—and you most certainly will when you learn to relax and let it do the work for you—then put the solution you have been given into effect immediately. Don't hesitate. Go ahead and solve your problem now that you know its correct solution.

How will the answer come to you? Most people receive their instructions or their guidance in terms of *feeling* what ought to be done. Remember that your conscious mind *thinks*; it uses logic and deductive reasoning. But your subconscious mind *feels* to get its answers.

So you will usually receive your instructions as hunches or intuition or flashes of inspiration. Many people have told me that when they receive guidance from their subconscious minds, they know their guidance is right, for they feel a mighty reassurance come upon them from a source outside of themselves.

Whether or not such a mighty reassurance comes to you, you will feel compelled to do things a certain way, even though sometimes such actions may seem completely ridiculous to you. Your instructions may defy logic and reason, but *unless they are obviously harmful to you or to someone else*, you should follow your hunches or your intuition to the letter. That is the way your subconscious mind will give you the solution to your problem.

For example, in the Ninth Chapter of John we read that Jesus spread a mud paste over a blind man's eyes and told him to go and wash it off in the pool of Siloam if he wanted to be cured. Now such an order sounds ridiculous, doesn't it? I'm sure it sounded ridiculous to the blind man, too, but nevertheless, he did as he was told, and the Scriptures say, "He went his way therefore, and washed, and came seeing." Had he not done as he was told to do, he would have still been blind. This is the same sort of obedience you should give to your subconscious mind if you want to get results from it.

I cannot tell you how long your subconscious mind will simmer away. But sooner or later, the idea—the answer you have been waiting for—will bubble to the top. And when it does, it usually surfaces with the speed of a hooked salmon. So you must be ready for it, no matter what you are doing—shaving, eating, driving the car, working, reading, or watching television.

You must be ready to write the answer down the moment the message comes to you. It will never come again as clearly as it does the first time. In fact, in most cases it will never come again. Your subconscious mind can be very stubborn. It figures once is enough; take it or leave it.

So when the idea does come, write down enough of it so it will be as clear and understandable a month or a year later as it is at that moment of time. I didn't always do that. Today, I have some cards in my files that have only one or two words written on them. I was so sure that I would never forget my code when I wrote the message down, but I've had some of those cards for years now, and I still don't know what they mean.

An example of how your answer might come to you

It took a famous and well-known writer of nonfiction books a long time to develop his present successful style and format.

"I was having trouble using examples to illustrate my point in my first book," he told me. "The publisher had pointed out that I needed lots of examples and case histories to add authenticity to my writing and prove my points. My editor said that this came easy for some writers, but hard for others. I guess I was a slow learner, for I just couldn't seem to get a handle on it.

"I thought about it for a long time and then I finally gave up and turned it over to my subconscious mind as you had suggested to get my answer. It took me several days, but I can remember distinctly where I was when I got my answer and exactly how it came to me.

"I was driving west on Sunshine Avenue and I was just across from the Holiday Bowling Lanes when a thought came to me as clearly as if a voice had spoken out loud. 'You do it this way,' the thought came to me, and then just as if I were reading a printed page right out of a book, I saw the format for using examples and case histories as clear as crystal. That was 15 books ago and I have used the same style successfully ever since."

Let me summarize this procedure for you now before going on to the next subject:

1. Identify your exact problem.

2. Determine the precise cause of your problem.

3. Figure out all the possible solutions.

4. Evaluate the possible solutions.

5. Pick the best solution with your thinking (conscious) mind. (If these five steps solve your problem, go to Step *6a*. If they do not, then go to Step *6b*, and then on to *Step 7*.)

6a. Put your solution into effect—take the necessary action.

6b. Turn all the information over to your subconscious mind so it can solve your problem for you.

7. When you receive the answer from your subconscious mind, act immediately upon the instructions that you receive.

This procedure I've just outlined for communicating with your subconscious mind is often more quickly grasped by a woman than by a man. You see, a woman has an intuitive or instinctive sixth sense to help her guide her actions. Not only that, a woman can anticipate a problem coming as easily as a man might smell a skunk. This intuitive sixth sense is the guidance a woman receives from her subconscious mind, even if she doesn't realize where it's really coming from.

How your subconscious mind can show you a better way of doing things

Your subconscious mind can help you just as the subconscious mind of the successful nonfiction writer I just told you about helped him. I must tell you, however, that creative ideas or inspiration will not come to you unless you first use your conscious mind to think intensely about the problem.

If you want to receive inspiration or an intuitive hunch about how to do something, you must first of all be deeply interested in solving a specific problem or finding a better way of doing things.

You must think about the problem, gather all the information about it that you can, consider all the possible courses of action just as I've already shown you. And, above all, you must have a burning desire, yes, even an overpowering obsession, to solve that problem. It is a maxim that desire is the first law of gain. Without that burning desire, nothing worthwhile can ever be achieved, no problem will ever be solved.

After you've defined and isolated your problem, secured all the facts and information that you can about it, seen in your imagination the desired end result, then turn everything over to your subconscious mind to get the solution for you. Further struggle and worry with your conscious mind will only delay the answer. Let me give you a concrete example of how well this method can work for you. I learned about this one on a trip I made through the west one year.

As I stood with other tourists staring in wide-eyed awe at the Grand Coulee, one of the world's largest dams—which is nearly a mile long and almost two football fields high—I wondered how it had been humanly possible to build such a tremendous structure. Then I heard the park guide say, "Had it not been for the imagination of a young construction engineer who refused to accept defeat, the Grand Coulee Dam might never have been built.

"You see, the engineers working on the project had run up against a seemingly unsolvable problem. They had reached a point where their normal construction methods would not work because of deep deposits of constantly shifting sand and mud.

"Tons of it poured into newly excavated areas; it tore out pilings and scaffoldings. All sorts of engineering techniques were tried without success. There seemed to be no possible answer to their problem and the situation began to look completely hopeless. In fact, some of the best engineering minds in the business were just about ready to give up building the dam.

"Then one of the engineers had an inspiration. 'When I woke up this morning, a strange idea was in my mind,' he said. 'I know it sounds crazy at first, but I think it will actually work. Let's drive pipes down through all that sand and mud. Then we can circulate a refrigerant through them and freeze the whole mess solid as a rock. When that's done, we won't have to worry about it coming down on top of us while we work.'

"So they tried his idea, almost as a last resort. In a short time, the unmanageable and shifting wet sand and mud had been frozen into one huge solid rock. They could have built a skyscraper on it if they had wanted to.

"So the Grand Coulee Dam came into existence and millions of people have benefited because one young engineer had a hunch and refused to accept defeat. Instead he acted as if it were impossible to fail, and complete success was the end result."

After I heard the park guide's story, I knew that the young engineer had gotten help from his subconscious mind to solve his problem, although he probably never realized where his idea actually came from.

How using the art of meditation can get the answer you need

Because of the influence of some Asian religious cults in recent years, some people think that meditation is associated with the occult and is actually unchristian. Nothing could be further from the truth. To meditate simply means to think or reflect deeply upon a particular subject.

The doctor who was our family's physician when I was a child always retired to his study after he had finished his lunch to meditate on his problem cases. "I receive the guidance I need from somewhere within me when I am faced with a difficult case," he told me later when I was older and went to him for advice before starting my college education at the University of Iowa.

"It is this daily dose of silence and meditation that I prescribe for myself that gives me the strength I need to help my patients. I could not survive without it.

"No matter what you decide to do for a living, young man, problems will come your way at times. You can cope with them if you will learn to relax in a quiet place, meditate, and wait for the right answers to come to you."

You, too, can use meditation to solve many of your problems. Select a quiet place where you will not be interrupted, clear your conscious mind of all worries and distractions, and listen for that "still small voice within" to give you the answer that you need.

Give yourself at least half an hour for your meditative session. Anything less than that will probably be of little use to you for it takes time to clear your conscious thinking mind completely so it will be receptive to the guidance you receive from your subconscious mind.

What does meditation actually do for you? It unclogs your conscious mind so the perfect answer to your problem can come through to you from your subconscious mind. If you feel that this answer is coming to you from a source outside yourself, say a higher power which most people choose to call God, that's fine. I have no argument whatever with that concept.

Dr. Emmet Fox, one of the most prolific and widely read spiritual writers of all time, says in effect that to meditate properly, you must stop thinking about your problem, whatever it is, and think about God instead. Dr. Fox says that if you will simply do this, the trouble will soon disappear. If this religious or spiritual approach will work for you in solving your problems, then, of course, by all means use it. Your answer, no matter what its origin or source, will still be transmitted to your conscious mind either by or through your subconscious mind.

When you are sure that you have your answer, simply go ahead and do what needs to be done. No matter how absurd or how ridiculous the answer might sound to you, unless it is obviously harmful to you or to someone else, you should follow your directions to the letter.

Remember the blind man who washed in the pool of Siloam or the young construction engineer whose inspiration resulted in the Grand Coulee Dam being built. Had they not followed their directions, they would both have failed to get the results that they wanted.

How sleeping on the problem can get results for you

Sometimes a period of meditation is not enough. At times sleeping on the problem is the only way you can get the answer that you need.

A certain businessman and close friend of mine, I'll just call him John, a few years ago was deeply in debt and on the verge of complete bankruptcy. After talking it over with me about how to use the subconscious mind to solve problems, he decided to try my system. As he told me later, he had nothing to lose and everything to gain. He began calling on his subconscious mind for help, using a technique that works well for many people.

"I began putting a blank note pad and a pencil by my bed," John said. "Very often I would wake up in the middle of the night with a solution to a problem and I would write down the answer. Sometimes in the morning I would find things on that pad that I couldn't even remember writing down. There were a lot of darned good ideas that came from my subconscious mind for me to use while I was sound asleep."

As John started putting these ideas to work, he found that his attitude about his business was changing from negative to positive. Evidently his enthusiasm rubbed off on his customers, for his business increased and soon he could face his creditors instad of ducking them.

"I just stopped worrying about my bills and left things up to my subconscious mind to take care of for me," John said. "Before too long all those problems that seemed so impossible to solve didn't seem so large anymore."

Today John is highly successful in his business. But he hasn't let his success change his system of writing things down during the night on his note pad. He still uses it.

A famous American novelist says this: "One of the most helpful discoveries I made long ago was that some power within me continues to work while I am sleeping, relaxing, or engaged in some other kind of work not even related to writing.

"When I'm having a problem with my story, I turn it over to this power to solve for me when I go to bed. I usually awaken in the morning to find a problem of technique, plot, or character, which had been troubling me, completely solved while I've been sleeping.

"I accept the answer I get without question for I have found that the judgment of this power—whatever it is—is infallible. Evidently it represents inherited instincts and the accumulation of all my experiences, none of which have been forgotten. I always trust the judgment of this power over any conclusions arrived at through a long process of thinking by my mind."

The unnamed power this novelist is using is his subconscious mind, although he evidently doesn't realize it. He just knows that something within him is helping him to solve his problems and find the answers that he needs.

This procedure of sleeping on the problem to get the solution from the subconscious mind works extremely well for many people. It could be the best procedure for you, too. It's up to you to experiment so you can find out for yourself. If you feel more comfortable using the religious approach to contact your subconscious mind, then do as a friend of mine does. As he puts it, he always sleeps with his mind open to God. He expects answers and he gets them.

How to get your conscious mind on the right frequency to receive your answer

Scientists have determined that the brain wave patterns vary greatly with the type of activity in which a person is engaged. The brain produces electrical energy that can be measured by an electroencephalograph (EEG). The rhythms of this brain energy are measured in cycles per second. Generally speaking, about 12 cycles per second and above are termed *Beta* waves; seven to 12 are *Alpha*; four to seven are *Theta*; three and below are called *Delta*.

When you are wide awake and going about your normal everyday tasks, you will be in Beta. When you are daydreaming, or just about to go to sleep, or just waking up in the morning, you are in Alpha. When you are fully asleep, you can be in Theta, Alpha, or Delta. Delta is the soundest sleep of all. The brain wave pattern is very slow, usually only one to three cycles per second. Delta is also the state the brain is in during anesthesia.

You will be in Theta most of the time while you are sleeping, although you can drift in and out of Alpha. Alpha is the state your subconscious mind uses to transmit messages to your conscious mind whether during the night while you are sleeping or during the day when you are engaged in meditation.

As you can see from this, you want to get into the Alpha state for the best results in meditation. The best way to do that is to sit relaxed in a comfortable chair in a quiet room with your eyes closed. To completely eliminate outside distractions or wayward thoughts, count backward from 100 to 1 very slowly. The principle here is almost like that of counting sheep to go to sleep, except you do not want to pass on into Delta or Theta. You want only to get into Alpha and stay there during your meditation.

As you practice this, you will soon be able to recognize the Alpha state and differentiate it from the Beta state. One of the things you will notice is that you will have a feeling of complete peace for you cannot bring feelings of anger and resentment from the Beta to the Alpha state. If these feelings of your conscious mind do intrude, you will immediately come out of Alpha and return to Beta. But persistence will pay off for you if you don't give up.

A good way to leave your feelings of anger and resentment behind is to do as Dr. Emmet Fox has suggested: think only about God. Do not try to form a picture of Him in your mind, for that would be impossible since no one knows what God really looks like. Instead, think about all the good characteristics He possesses: wisdom, knowledge, truth, love, compassion, and so on. This method will help you keep anger and resentment out of your meditative state.

Alpha is also the best state in which to practice the art of mental imagery, psycho-pictography, or visualizing what it is that you want. The better you learn to visualize, the more powerful will become the answers from your subconscious mind.

You can also use the Alpha state to remember things that your conscious mind seems to have forgotten. Although I have a cabinet in the garage in which to keep my tools, I must admit that I often neglect to put a hammer, a screwdriver, or a pair of pliers back where they belong.

Now you know nothing is ever really lost for me—it is just misplaced temporarily. It will always be in the exact spot where I left it. I have found countless numbers of misplaced tools in the identical spots where my subconscious mind told me to look.

When I can't find a specific tool that I want, I simply sit down, close my eyes, go immediately into Alpha (which is easy for me to do after so much practice and experience), and within a few moments the answer will come and I will be led immediately to the correct spot.

For instance, a few days ago I couldn't find a small hand-saw I wanted to use. But after a few moments in Alpha, I saw it clearly in my mind's eye. It was on top of the carport where I'd been repairing a leaky plastic pipe for my swimming pool's solar heating unit a few days before.

Many others to whom I have taught this method tell me they've found such diversified "lost" items as tools, airline tickets, keys, business papers and plans, glasses, wallets, jewelry, and so on.

How to make your subconscious mind a personal and intimate friend

You can make your subconscious mind the most valuable friend you will ever have. All you need do is talk to it just as you would talk to another person. Of course, it is wise to do this when you are alone. Otherwise, you might be regarded as a bit eccentric, to say the least.

I, myself, have no trouble whatever in carrying on a conversation with my subconscious mind. Admittedly, I have an advantage in some respects in this. You see, I was born and raised on an Iowa farm five miles from the closest town. I was an only child and there were no children my age close by with whom I could play. So I learned to talk with myself early in life and never considered it strange or abnormal to do so. Besides, talking to yourself is actually only thinking out loud and there's nothing wrong with that.

So I talk to my subconscious mind just as I might be talking to some individual to whom I'm giving orders. And I never have any doubts or fears of any sort that it will not do as I have told it to do.

For instance, if I get a bit of indigestion, I simply instruct my subconscious mind to tell my stomach to settle down and act naturally. I do the same thing with any other physical ailment that I might have now and then. These are extremely rare, though, for I have ordered my subconscious mind to keep me in good health, and it has done so for many, many years.

For a long time now I have not used an alarm clock. If I have to get up early for some reason or another, I merely tell my subconscious mind to wake me at five or six, and it has always done so. It has never failed me yet.

Now let's get on to the next chapter where I will show you how your subconscious mind uses the power of imagination and mental pictures to achieve success for you.

How Your Subconscious Mind Uses the Power of Imagination to Achieve Success for You

3

Today we have transistors in our radios, our television sets, and our stereo systems that replace the old-fashioned vacuum tube. Why? Well, transistors do not produce heat as vacuum tubes do, so therefore they do not burn out. They are virtually trouble-free and will last indefinitely. But that doesn't really say why at all, now does it? Then why?

Because someone used his imagination and came up with a better idea.

Every invention you can think of—from the first crude wheel to the intricate and highly sophisticated control system of the space shuttle—had its beginnings in the deep, dark recesses of the subconscious mind.

A tiny seed of thought was planted in a brain furrow. It was plowed under by the conscious mind and allowed to germinate for a while. Then it was watered and fertilized by the subconscious mind, and suddenly one day it blossomed into full flower. And all of us benefited because someone came up with a better idea of how to do something. Imagination is the golden key that will unlock the door to the abundant life for all mankind.

THE TREMENDOUS BENEFITS TO BE GAINED BY USING YOUR IMAGINATION

1. You'll discover new and better ways of doing things.

2. You can save time, labor, and money when you find new and better ways of doing things and put them into effect.

3. If you're in business, you'll increase your profit margin and be able to make more money for yourself.

4. If you're in a company or corporation, you can gain promotion and advancement to a better position.

5. You can discover solutions to your personal problems when you use your creative imagination.

Techniques You Can Use to Gain These Tremendous Benefits

How to use your imagination to get whatever you want

First of all, it is important for you to know that your subconscious mind cannot tell the difference between a real experience and one that you imagine. It reacts automatically to the information you program into it by your conscious mind. Your subconscious mind reacts, not only to what is actually true, but also to what you imagine.

You do not have to have had some experience to program your subconscious mind effectively. Of all the creatures on this earth, man is the only one who does not need to depend upon past experience to control his future. Another way of saying this is that man is the only one of God's creations who is allowed to finish the act of creation himself.

Your subconscious mind will store your emotional fantasies as reality. For instance, if you see yourself as a tremendously successful salesperson making $100,000 or more a year, and if you can actually believe this is possible, you are programming your subconscious mind with your imagination to bring your fantasy into reality.

You can visualize with your conscious mind all these good things that you want. And when you program your desires into your subconscious mind believing that you can have them—or better yet, *believing that you already have them*—your subconscious mind will go to work for you to devise the methods that will make your fantasy come true.

Some of the most helpful suggestions Jesus Christ gave mankind had to do with improving the quality of this life. Jesus well understood that our thoughts influence our physical circumstances. Time and again He said, "Ask and it shall be given unto you . . . seek and ye shall find . . . if thou canst believe, all things are possible . . . as thou hast believed, so be it done unto you."

You, too, can have whatever you can visualize if you believe that it is possible. A new car, a bigger house, a better job, a happier home life, all these can be yours. Your subconscious mind will react automatically to give you whatever you program into it, either real or imagined.

It is important to point out to you here that your subconscious mind will not take the trouble to work for you if you do not believe in it. Next, it is also highly important that in transmitting your message to your subconscious mind, you should do so in the spirit that the work has *already been done.*

Thus, while it is necessary for you to feel and think you are going to be successful, it is important to go one step further and actually *see yourself as already being successful,* either in the performance of some selected task or as actually occupying the position that you want.

How to use mental pictures to program your subconscious mind

I know you have seen actors and actresses on the screen and on television portraying grief so vividly that you almost became convinced that they were not acting, but were actually grief-stricken. I have had the opportunity to talk to some of these people and have asked them how they can portray sadness and grief so realistically.

Each one of them told me something along these lines: "I think back to some horribly sad incident in my past life—the death of my father or mother, the loss of a brother or sister—and recreate the entire scene again in my mind. When this sad mood is re-established, I am then ready to act grief-stricken in my acting role, tears and all."

I'm sure you've created pictures in your mind's eye after you've gone to bed and before you go to sleep. If you're like I am, you can create extremely detailed pictures on your mental screen. You can also do the same when you're relaxing in an easy chair just daydreaming.

The important point here is that you should project mental pictures that will help you gain your goals in life rather than just idle fantasizing or daydreaming. Let me give you a concrete, practical example of how to use this technique properly.

A friend of mine, Al J., is an investment counselor for a large brokerage firm. Al had been trying to sell one quite wealthy individual some tax-exempt bonds, but he was mentally afraid of his prospect, so he'd never been able to succeed with this one man.

"I know I could sell him if I could just get rid of my unreasonable fear of him, but he scares me to death," Al told me. "I just don't know how to get over this ridiculous fear I have of him."

I knew the man Al was referring to. He is a physically overpowering person with thick eyebrows, a constant frown, and a growling voice that can intimidate people who are easily frightened. But I also knew that he liked people who were not cowed by his heavy-handed manner.

"Al, why don't you try this approach with him," I said. "You know he's not going to harm you physically in spite of his mean and threatening appearance. So why don't you picture him in your mind's eye as someone who's always extremely friendly, say a minister or a priest. You know they are friendly with people so you can feel completely at ease with him."

I saw Al a few weeks later and he was bubbling over with enthusiasm. "I did as you suggested, Jim," he said. "I pictured him in my mind as a priest with his white collar on backward. My mental picture of him evidently carried over into my voice, my attitude, and my sales approach, for his reaction was a complete reversal of what it had been before. He invested $25,000 with me as a 'starter' as he put it, and he wants me to call back on him every month."

If you're in business or in sales and you have a tough nut to crack, just as Al had, make up your own mental picture of that individual and see how your imagination can help you out. I've also known young trial lawyers who used this method successfully when they were up against someone with experience, background, and talent that were far greater than theirs.

So try this yourself; I know you will be most happy with the results that you get. The better you learn to visualize and use mental pictures, the more powerful and dependable your subconscious mind will become.

How you help your subconscious mind by using mental pictures

Your subconscious mind can operate in only one way. Since it is a goal-seeking mechanism, it must be given a goal to reach, an objective to attain. You must see clearly in your conscious mind exactly what you want before your subconscious mind can go to work for you. When you know specifically what you want to gain, your subconscious mind's creativity will take over and do the job for you much better than you could possibly do with your conscious mind by using willpower.

So instead of trying to achieve your goal by using iron-jawed determination and willpower, simply turn things over to your subconscious mind. Then relax, stop worrying and fretting, picture to yourself mentally exactly what it is you want to achieve, and let the creative power of your subconscious mind take over and do the job for you.

You are not relieved from effort and work, a point I will discuss at greater length when I tell you how imagination and initiative work together; but for now, let me say that when you combine the two, they will take you in a straight line toward your goal without any futile meandering.

How to use the mirror technique to program your subconscious mind

Top-notch salespeople, professional public speakers, television evangelists, politicians—all these practice their techniques in front of a mirror to become successful. Winston Churchill, for instance, never made a speech of major importance without first rehearsing it in front of the mirror.

One of the most successful insurance salesmen America has ever known never called upon a prospect without first giving his sales presentation to his own reflection in the mirror. Every salesperson has heard the idea that if you can convince yourself first of the valuable benefits you have to offer, then you can always convince the other person.

When I was in the army way back in World War II, I commanded a training company for a time while stationed at Fort Leonard Wood, Missouri, where raw recruits fresh from civilian life were turned into proud professional soldiers in just 16 weeks.

When a soldier went on pass, he had to sign out in a company register in the orderly room. Before he left, he saw his reflection in a full length mirror on the door. Above the mirror were the words, "You are a soldier in the best army in the world. Act like one . . . look like one . . . be one."

I have watched hundreds of young men, who a few short weeks before arrived not caring about their dress or their personal appearance, stand tall before that mirror, look sharp, check every last detail of their reflection, and then turn away with a proud smile of satisfaction with what they saw.

While at Fort Leonard Wood, I also saw my battalion commander, a lieutenant colonel, use this mirror technique to sober himself up after he'd had too much to drink at a regimental party at the officers club.

I saw Colonel Fred C. get up from a table in the bar and stagger his way to the washroom. Thinking that he might fall and injure himself, I followed him to see if I could be of any assistance. When I opened the door to the washroom, he was standing in front of the mirror, holding onto the sink with both hands and talking to his reflection. I heard him say, "Fred, you fool, sober up. You're making an ass out of yourself in front of not only the regimental commander, but also, your own officers as well. You are sober . . . you are sober . . . you are cold sober . . . straighten up and fly right."

As he watched his reflection in the mirror, he kept repeating aloud that he was sober, and in a few moments I saw an actual physical change taking place in his body.

He took his hands off the sink, straightened up, and stood fully erect. His drunken look slowly vanished, his glassy eyes cleared, and his speech became coherent. Then he turned to walk back to his table, apparently completely sober, although his face was still slightly flushed. I watched for a while longer, but he remained sober and in complete control of himself and his actions.

How can you use the mirror technique yourself? Well, one way is to face your reflection each morning and say, "I am a successful person. I am a worthwhile person. No one can keep me from gaining my goals or achieving my objectives."

As you say these things, believing fully that they are true, stand fully erect, pull in your stomach, stick out your chest, and hold your head high. Feel a sense of power, strength, and determination coursing through your body. As you look into your eyes, tell yourself and believe it that you are going to get everything you want out of life.

The mirror technique is an extremely reliable method that you can use to strengthen your belief in your innate natural abilities and intensify your enthusiasm and perseverance for getting ahead.

How to establish a creative climate for your subconscious mind

One of the principles super salespeople follow is this: *Find a need and fill it*. The same principle applies to your subconscious mind. Unless there is a need for it to work for you, it never will. You must give it a goal to reach, an objective to achieve before it will go into action.

If you could coax a fish to jump out of the water into your frying pan, no one would ever figure out a better way to catch fish. There'd be no reason to do so. So the most important incentive in getting your subconscious mind to give you a new idea is pressure, a requirement, a need or an urgency for getting the job done.

For instance, hunger produced the club and then the bow and arrow. Within reason, the pressure of deadlines and time limits helps to bring out a person's best creative powers.

The pressure of war, for example, caused medical science to find answers and cures far faster than ordinary. "Medicine today has advanced much further than it would have otherwise," says Dr. Rodney Charles, a university professor of internal medicine. "And all because of war. We had no time to spend in leisurely research. We needed everything yesterday."

Unless this sense of urgency exists, your subconscious mind will not come up with new ideas for you. It will not try to figure out a better way of doing things, unless you've given it a valid reason to do so. Here is a six-step procedure you can use to establish that necessary creative climate for your subconscious mind.

1. Know exactly what it is you want to accomplish. Be specific about the goal you want to reach, the objective you want to attain.

2. Believe in your heart of hearts that your subconscious mind will give you the answer you want and need.

3. Gather up all the available facts you have on the subject.

4. Feed all those facts into your subconscious mind along with your request for an answer.

5. Relax. Wait patiently and watch diligently for the answer to your question or the solution to your problem.

6. Take immediate action when you receive the answer from your subconscious mind.

Although all six steps are important in this process, unless you take action as required in the last step, all the preceding work has been wasted. Not only that, you'll soon find that if you don't take the action your subconscious mind has given you, it will simply stop working for you. It will reach the conclusion that you are not at all serious about your requests for help, so it won't give you any more fresh thoughts or new ideas to use. I'll discuss that idea with you next.

Why imagination and initiative go hand in hand

In business and industry, good usable labor-saving and money-making ideas are hard to come by. Not that people don't come up with good ideas. They do, but they don't follow up and develop them. In effect, creative ability is two percent inspiration and 98 percent perspiration. And in spite of all the fancy deodorants we have, the average person doesn't like to sweat. For instance,

"I just had the most brilliant idea!" Jack Jones exclaims. His face glows with enthusiasm; his eyes sparkle with imagination, but only momentarily. "But it would take . . . and then there would be . . . and the boss wouldn't . . . and I couldn't . . . forget it. It wasn't such a good idea after all, I guess."

And so a fresh new idea dies before it was even decently born. Jack had the two percent inspiration, all right. His subconscious mind gave him that. But he just didn't have that 98 percent perspiration it takes to develop that momentary spark of creative genius. He had the imagination, but not the initiative to follow through on his idea.

Imagination without initiative would more properly be called idle daydreaming. Daydreams have no goals. They have no root or purpose, no objective or goal to achieve. They are only wishful thinking, which not only accomplishes nothing, but also actually gets in the way of useful imagination.

The best way to actively use your imagination and not just coast along daydreaming is to know exactly what it is that you want to get done. Then follow up with the remaining five steps of that six-step procedure I gave you to establish the necessary creative climate in which your subconscious mind can work.

Let me sum up this section by saying that imagination plus initiative—*the power of commencing*—makes the difference between the thinker who does something and the daydreamer who accomplishes nothing.

Where all great ideas come from

Inventions, great musical compositions, poetry, fiction, and all other ideas for original accomplishment come from a person's subconscious mind.

You, too, can be just as creative. You may not be an inventor as such, a composer of music, or a writer of best-selling novels, but you can still use the hidden power of your subconscious mind to come up with a better way of doing things no matter what your line of work is.

Inventors, writers, composers, and poets, none of these have a monopoly on creativity. All you need do to be creative yourself is to give your subconscious mind the thought or the raw material it needs to go to work for you, keep it going with a deep-rooted desire for successful accomplishment, and you will get the results that you want. Let me give you a specific example of that:

A wholesale nursery owner here in Florida, Bill Sanders, has a large number of plants, shrubs, and trees spread out over several acres They have to be watered every day. Bill became irritated because he was constantly having to replace the sprinkler heads. Not only was it the cost, but it was also the time and the inconvenience of constantly having to replace the sprinkler heads that finally got to Bill.

"Artesian wells here in Florida are extremely hard on ordinary metal sprinkler heads because the water is so high in sulphur and other organic materials that cause decay," Bill said. "Florida water is also high in salt content which corrodes metal easily. And because most sprinklers have rotary bases with pinholes, there are constant maintenance problems because the sand and shell content in the water clogs the bushings."

So Bill went to work on the problem and turned it over to his subconscious mind to solve for him. Soon the idea came to him for a new sprinkler head that was all nylon rather than metal. Now he has no more maintenance problems at his nursery with his sprinkler system.

When a manufacturer saw his new sprinklers, he bought the rights and pays Bill a royalty on every one that is manufactured. The first year more than 100,000 units were sold and now manufacturing rights have been granted in Canada and England. Bill says he's making enough money from that one idea that he could quit the nursery business. But he won't simply because he enjoys what he's doing.

As you can see from this, you don't have to be an inventor to come up with a new way of doing things. All you need is a problem to solve and who doesn't have problems?

Don't let others turn off your creativity

Ninety-five people out of a hundred think like this: "We've been doing it this way for as long as I can remember. So it must be the best way. Why should we change it?"

I'd be the first to admit that I'm a strong believer in the principle of "If it ain't broke, don't fix it." But by the same token, I'm always willing to accept change, just as long as it isn't change for the sake of change. If that change will result in a better way of doing things, then I'm all for it.

But most people don't like change at all. They resent progress. Remember the phrase, "that old-time religion"? People also protested the automobile for they felt that horses were good enough for transportation. And many more protested against the airplane than against the automobile. The saying of that day was, "If man were meant to fly, God would have given him wings." And so it goes, on and on. But as Dr. Von Braun, the gifted German scientist, once said, "Man belongs wherever man wants to go."

The best way to keep others from turning off your creativity is to keep your transactions with your subconscious mind a deep secret all to yourself. If you tell others what you are doing, many won't understand and will think you're completely off your rocker, to put it mildly. They'll criticize you, even ridicule you. Criticism and ridicule from others can quickly and completely destroy your confidence in yourself and in your subconscious mind's ability to help you.

So the best way to keep others from planting negative ideas in your conscious mind, which will then be transferred to your subconscious mind, is to tell them absolutely nothing of your techniques, your methods, or your procedures.

I have found, for example, when I talk to someone about a proposed writing project or ask a person for an opinion on it, I scatter my forces. I lose my close connection with my subconscious mind, and more often than not, I find I have to start all over again.

So today I won't even tell my wife of more than 45 years anything at all about a current writing project that I'm working on, not even the title. The first time she knows what I've been doing is when the published book is put in her hands.

How your imagination can work against you

Suppose you are in bed at night sound asleep and you wake suddenly, sure that you've heard a strange noise out in the kitchen. Immediately your heart starts to pound wildly and you are almost afraid to breathe for fear the burglar might hear you.

Do you know what has actually happened within your body? Your fight or flight mechanism has gone into action automatically for you. Your blood pressure is increased and your heart rate speeds up. There is a marked increase in blood flow to your arms and legs; more adrenalin is pumped into your blood stream. All this because of a noise you heard at night out in the kitchen.

But when you finally get up the courage to check, after you heard nothing more for a long time, you find there was no burglar after all. Only a bag of trash that had been placed too close to the edge of the counter had finally fallen off breaking a bottle that made the clatter you heard.

That's how easily negative ideas can be fed into your subconscious mind by your conscious mind to keep it from working properly for you. Let me give you another example:

I have a screened-in pool and leaves gather on the screen roof above next to the house and rot. Then when it rains, a brown residue drips down and leaves streaked stains on the house wall.

So every so often I take a plank 2" by 8" by 12 feet long and carry it up to the roof so I can lower it by ropes to the screened-in roof where it rests on strong steel beams that are four feet apart. Then I go over the side of the roof and get on that plank so I can reach the leaves and dispose of them.

Now when that plank is lying on the patio floor, I can walk back and forth on it easily, never stepping off of it and never losing my balance. When it's in position over the pool screen it's just as solid on those steel beams as it is on the patio. And even though that plank is a full eight inches wide, do you think I can walk upright on it then? Are you kidding? I'm on my hands and knees hanging on for dear life, afraid I'll lose my balance, fall through the screen, and into the pool. Who says that imagination isn't the most powerful force in the world?

So please remember that negative thinking will always produce negative results, but positive programming of your subconscious mind will always produce positive results.

Let me close this chapter by quoting the French writer and essayist, Montaigne, who said in his latter years, "My life has been filled with terrible misfortunes, most of which never happened!" That's exactly what negative thinking can do to you, too.

And now on to Chapter 4, where you will see why the output of your subconscious mind will always equal its input, and, really, why it could be no other way.

Why the Output of Your Subconscious Mind Always Equals Its Input

4

If you've ever had your own garden, you know full well that if you plant tomatoes, you will raise tomatoes. If you sow onions, then you will grow onions. We all understand this natural law and we work with it. Unfortunately, many people do not understand that the same exact principle applies to the subconscious mind. But it could be no other way. Let me show you precisely what I mean by that.

Good thoughts and good actions can never produce bad results. By the same token, bad thoughts and bad actions can never produce good results. The same law applies here as in the natural world. The output of your subconscious mind always equals its input.

If you have been programming your subconscious mind with the wrong kinds of thoughts—for instance, "I'm a failure . . . only people with college degrees are successful, and I don't have one . . . I can't do that"—you are going to get back exactly what you've been programming into your subconscious mind: *failure*.

I want to use this chapter to show you how to program your subconscious mind with the proper material, for when you do that,

YOU'LL GAIN THESE OUTSTANDING BENEFITS

1. When you know how to program your subconscious mind with the proper input, you'll become successful in whatever you do.

2. You'll see how the proper attitude can influence the output of your subconscious mind for the better.

3. You'll learn the most effective ways to improve your memory, a most valuable benefit.

4. You'll see how you can improve your performance when you use the 30-day test for self-improvement.

5. You'll learn a six-step program that's a quick short-cut to success.

Techniques You Can Use to Gain These Outstanding Benefits

How your subconscious mind works like a computer

First of all, your subconscious mind does exactly as it is programmed or directed to do by your conscious mind. It does not function haphazardly or at random with no purpose on its own. It carries out the instructions that are given to it by your conscious mind.

Remember that your subconscious mind is neutral. It places no value judgments on what is programmed into it by your conscious mind. Moral judgments are the responsibility of your conscious mind to determine. If what your conscious mind has decided to do is immoral or illegal, your subconscious mind will not act as a deterrent to that decision. It will carry out your orders to the letter, be those orders legal or illegal, moral or immoral.

Secondly, your subconscious mind will return to your conscious mind exactly what has been programmed into its memory banks. I want to discuss that point more fully with you now. I have already likened your subconscious mind to a backyard garden and said that if you planted tomatoes, you would raise tomatoes, and that if you sowed onions, you would reap onions. But both of these are good crops and could be considered comparable to good thoughts planted in your subconscious mind by your conscious mind. So let me carry this comparison a bit further this way:

Let's look at that backyard garden again. Now you have a choice as to what you are going to plant in it. You may plant whatever you choose to in the ground. The ground doesn't care. It's all up to you to decide that. Let's suppose you have two seeds in your hand. One is a seed of corn, the other, belladonna, a deadly poison.

You dig two holes in the ground and plant both seeds: one, belladonna, the other, corn. You cover up the holes with dirt, you water, fertilize, and take care of your planting. What will happen? Well, a small child could tell you that. The ground will return to you exactly what was planted in it. That is a law of nature, invaluable and unbreakable. The soil will return poison in just as much abundance as it will return corn.

Your conscious mind and your subconscious mind work in exactly the same way. If your conscious mind plants anger, resentment, envy, failure, defeat, and other negative thoughts in your subconscious mind, you will get back precisely what you have planted. As you can easily see from this example, *a person does literally become what he thinks about.*

If you are going to control your life, then, you must first control your thoughts. You must be extremely careful what you think about, for your subconscious mind never forgets what you program into it, either good or bad. It is your memory bank and that is the next subject that I want to take up with you.

How your subconscious mind acts as your memory bank

Everything that has ever happened to you, all you have read, studied, been told, seen, or experienced is retained in the memory banks of your subconscious mind in complete detail. Information storage has to take place in your subconscious mind. It would be absolutely impossible for your conscious mind to act as your memory bank and remember all past events. If we were to be simultaneously aware in our conscious minds of all the millions and millions of pieces of information stored in the memory banks of our subconscious minds, we would be completely unable to function. We would quickly go insane from the bombardment of information.

Now nothing that has ever happened to you is ever forgotten. What has been programmed into your subconscious mind is never removed. However, since much of that information is not required at all times to allow your conscious mind to function properly, it is not allowed to surface until it is needed for one reason or another.

A brilliant neurosurgeon and scientist proved by his experiments that past events—which the patient thought were completely forgotten—came back to the person's conscious mind vividly when an electric probe was used to stimulate those areas of the brain that house the memory banks of the subconscious mind.

For instance, one patient remembered being with some childhood friends whom he had not thought about for years and years. He could recall what they were doing and even what they were wearing. He could actually hear them talking and laughing. The amazing thing was that not only did he recall the event in his conscious mind when the memory banks of his subconscious mind in the brain were touched with the electric probe, but also he seemed to be reliving the experience.

Hypnotism can also help the conscious mind recall events that have been programmed into its subconscious mind, but that seem to have been forgotten. For example, in Chicago, two men held up a grocery store. A young couple was standing in front of the store when the two men ran out, jumped into a car, and drove away. When questioned by the police, neither one of this couple was able to remember the license plate of the car.

They both agreed to be hypnotized to see if they could then recall the license number. A hypnotist was called in by the police and each person's conscious mind was regressed under hypnotism to the time of the robbery. When hypnotized, both the man and woman were then able to remember the license number of the car, which had been automatically recorded in the memory banks of their subconscious minds. The robbers were then apprehended by the police.

In an example closer to home, I have a dog which was given to me to keep by our youngest son more than 12 years ago when he came to Florida to live. Larry had gotten the dog when it was a puppy, only a few weeks old. He had the dog for about a year before he moved to Orlando and into an apartment where pets were not allowed. So the dog became ours to care for.

Larry would visit us several times a year and each time he came the dog nearly went into orbit with joy. But the last time Larry came to see us, the dog had gone blind in both eyes and was also nearly deaf.

When Larry came up to Snapper, he did not say a word, but instead, sat down in a chair beside the dog and began to pet him. Snapper sniffed and smelled Larry's hand, then his clothes, and immediately began to cry and whimper and wag his tail with joy.

Even though he couldn't see or hear our son, his sense of smell immediately told him who the visitor was. His subconscious mind's memory banks were still working through his sense of smell, even though he was blind and nearly deaf. I had often heard that a dog never forgets its first master, and after seeing that incident, I firmly believe it.

As you can see from these three examples, nothing is ever forgotten that is programmed into your subconscious mind. Some events may seem hard to recall for reasons that I will discuss later, but before I do that, I want to tell you about the different kinds of memory storage in your subconscious mind.

The three different kinds of memory storage in your subconscious mind

As I mentioned to you previously, everything that has ever happened to you, all you have read, studied, been told, seen, or experienced is retained in the memory banks of your subconscious mind in complete detail. All this recorded information can be divided into three main kinds of storage: *experiential, word,* and *attitude or conceptual* which is derived from an interpretation of the first two.

1. *Experiential storage* in your subconscious mind comes from everything that has ever happened to you, everything you've been told, everything you've seen, heard, smelled, or tasted. Remember, too, that an imagined experience is just as real to your subconscious mind as an actual event that took place, for it cannot tell the difference between reality and fantasy.

2. *Word storage* in your subconscious mind is derived from everything you've read or studied and your understanding of the meaning of individual words.

3. *Attitude or conceptual storage* is your subconscious mind's interpretation of the first two storage systems. For example, if someone were to describe a bird to you, but never mentioned the actual word, *bird,* you would still know exactly what he was talking about.

Or if a person were to discuss perseverance, enthusiasm, success, failure, love, anger, resentment, your understanding of words and your actual experience causes your subconscious mind to play back to your conscious mind a picture that conveys the attitudes or concepts you have of such terms. Your concept of life and your actions toward people will be based upon the attitudes you have programmed into your subconscious mind for permanent storage and memory recall.

Why certain events are hard to recall

Usually, something cannot be recalled by your conscious mind from your subconscious mind's memory banks for one of three reasons:

1. *The event is distasteful, embarrassing, or painful to your conscious mind.* Sometimes, the past event is so distasteful or so painful that your conscious mind simply blocks out the memory and will not allow it to be recalled from your subconscious mind. It simply refuses to relive the experience over again.

Incest or rape are two examples where the victim is not the perpetrator. In other cases, where a person has committed some act completely foreign to his nature, his conscious mind refuses to recall the incident. An example would be an illegal or immoral act performed by a person while under the influence of drugs or alcohol.

2. *Your conscious mind does not consider an incident to be important* at the time it occurs, and, therefore, no strong impression is transmitted to your subconscious mind. This is not to say that your subconscious mind does not record and remember the incident. It does, but it is only looked at as trivia for your conscious mind placed no great importance on it.

No two people will attach the same importance to whatever is happening. My wife and I have been married for more than 45 years, yet she will recall vividly incidents that I just don't seem to remember at all. By the same token, I will recall events that escape her memory completely. The simple reason for this is the amount of importance each of us attaches to the experience.

3. *Too much is happening all at once*, as in a robbery or a car accident. Your conscious mind cannot concentrate on all the details at the same time. It tries to absorb everything that is happening, and as a result, literally nothing is absorbed. That is why when eyewitnesses of an accident or a robbery are questioned, there are so many conflicting or different versions of the same incident.

How you can improve your subconscious mind's memory

You can use three specific methods to improve your memory. These are: (1) concentration on the event; (2) use of association; (3) learning to be more observant. Let me discuss each one of these in detail with you now.

1. *Concentrate on the event.* When you concentrate on what is taking place, you can absorb better with your conscious mind, a deeper imprint is made on the neurons in that part of the brain that houses your subconscious mind, and recall is much easier. Being able to concentrate intently and keep your conscious mind from jumping around from one distraction to another is important for a better memory.

Many times lack of concentration can be merely a bad habit that is a carryover from your youth. During your school days if you daydreamed and let your mind wander when you should have been studying, this may have been the beginning of a bad habit pattern. In such a case, your subconscious mind concludes that the material is not important so it makes very little effort to record the information. Only a shallow imprint is made.

To correct this bad habit, force your conscious mind to concentrate totally on the point you want to remember and completely disregard distracting and extraneous input.

2. *Use of association.* Memory courses always plug the idea of association for better recall. Some people try to use rhyming words like *myth* with *Smith*, *bones* for *Jones*, that sort of thing to remember names. That's fine as long as you don't forget the rhyming word.

I use a different system entirely. When I am introduced to a person, I always repeat his name aloud to impress my subconscious mind with it. Then if it's quite different, I ask him to spell it. And I always ask what the ethnic derivation of the name is, French, Italian, Polish, Hungarian, and so on. By the time I'm through with all that, I couldn't possibly forget his name. People don't mind my questions a bit. After all, a person's name is one of his most important possessions. I'm simply feeding his ego by my interest in him.

My wife isn't as good at remembering names as I am. But she always knows the color of the person's eyes and hair. She observes these two points and remembers them and thinks it odd that I do not. But it's merely a matter of emphasis. I place my emphasis on names. She places hers on appearance, which is, I believe, the more feminine approach.

3. *Learn to be more observant.* One of the best ways to become more observant is to avoid mental distractions. Also, it would be wise to follow the system of *who, what, when, where, why, and how.* Police are specially trained to note the physical appearance of people, the kind of clothes they are wearing, that sort of thing.

A good way to practice this procedure is to look at a person for 10 seconds, starting from the head and moving down to the feet, observing everything you can see as you go: color of hair, color of eyes, complexion, scars or blemishes on the face, if any; type of clothing, color and cut of coat, rings, watches, trousers, skirts, color and kind of shoes, estimated height and weight. Then turn your eyes away and see how well you do at remembering all these details. If you practice this method carefully, within a week or so you will find that your powers of observation will have increased tremendously and so will your power of recall.

How having an excellent memory can help you

Having an excellent memory is not only of importance in connection with school and studies, but it is also of great value in your work and your everyday life. In some lines of work, such as acting or singing, for example, it is of extreme importance to be able to memorize easily.

Our three children are all professional musicians and entertainers and know by memory hundreds of songs. They perform together in a family group known quite appropriately as *The Family Tree*. Our two sons Bob and Larry—Bob plays a guitar and Larry a bass—are required to remember not only the words of the song, but also all the notes to be played on their musical instruments as well.

One way to force yourself to be more observant and concentrate on the subject at hand is to follow the advice of a mail-order millionaire, Mr. E. Joseph Cossman, who said, "Look at each piece of correspondence, think about it, make a decision, pass it along for action, file it if necessary, or destroy it . . . but never, never handle the same piece of paper twice. Your fidelity to this one rule will always keep your desk clear."

Not only will this keep your desk clear, but it will also give you an incentive for developing a better memory. If you box yourself into a corner by not allowing yourself to look at the same piece of paper twice, you will have no choice but to concentrate on the subject at hand and develop a better memory.

How to program your subconscious mind with the right concepts

You cannot program your subconscious mind with thoughts of anger, hate, and resentment toward people and expect to be loved and respected in return. Your deeply ingrained anger, hate, and resentment will be quite evident in your relationships with people. If you are rude to others, they will be rude to you. If you are hostile toward them, they will be hostile toward you.

If this is the sort of reaction you've been getting from people, then you need to change your attitude and program your subconscious mind with thoughts of kindness, love, and courtesy toward others, for as you think, so shall you become.

You will find that as you alter your thoughts and attitudes toward people, then other people will alter their thoughts and attitudes toward you. That point is easily proven, for. . . . .

* If you are kind to others, they will be kind to you.
* If you are courteous to others, they will be courteous to you.
* If you are friendly with others, they will be friendly with you.

In dealing with others, you will always see your attitude reflected in the other person's behavior. It is almost as if you were looking at yourself in a mirror. You need not say a word to influence the other person. A smile is contagious. Try it; you'll like it. Not only that, it beats the heck out of anger, hate, and resentment. Besides, you'll find it's a lot easier on your stomach, too.

How to program your subconscious mind for self-improvement

Here's an excellent way to prove to yourself that the output of your subconscious mind always equals its input. I would like to ask you to write down on a card what it is that you want more than anything else in life. It could be more money. Maybe you'd like to increase your income or make a specific amount of money. It could be a new house that you want. Or it might be a certain position in your company. Perhaps you want a happier home life, a better relationship with your wife and children.

Whatever it is, write down on your card exactly what it is that you want. Make sure that it is a concrete and specific goal that is clearly defined. Do not show your card to anyone or tell anyone what your goal is.

Look at your card no less than three times a day, morning, noon, and night. Think about what you want as often as you can throughout the day in a cheerful and relaxed manner. Do not be anxious or worried about reaching your goal.

As you look at your card or as you think about what is written on it, remember that *you must become what you think about*, and since you are thinking about what you want, you know that it will soon be yours. To tell the truth, it is already yours the moment you write it down and begin to think about it. Look at the abundance around you and realize that you are entitled to this world's riches as much as anyone else is. It is yours for the mere asking.

Now for an extremely important point for you to remember. It is a fact that *fear is always on the opposite side of the coin of desire*. That is to say that people want to gain something, but they are always afraid that they won't get it. Unfortunately, many persons concentrate on the fear that they will not attain something rather than on the desire that they will. To keep that from happening to you, I'd like to ask you to stop thinking about whatever it is that you fear, and instead, concentrate entirely on what it is that you want.

Try this test for 30 days. Control your thoughts as never before. If for one moment you think about the fear of failure or the fear that you will not attain the goal you have written on your card, force that fear out of your mind and concentrate entirely on your goal alone. Another way of saying this would be to *concentrate on the solution, not on the problem.* If you will concentrate on your goal and keep the fear of failure out of your mind, your subconscious mind will take care of the rest for you. Its powers will supply the answers you need to achieve your objective.

One final point about your goal is this. It should be realistic so you will not become discouraged when it is not obtained overnight. Don't expect to become a millionaire at the end of 30 days. Your goal must be reasonable.

If money is your goal, as it is with so many of us, I can tell you that your success will always be measured by the service that you give to others. Money is merely a means of measuring this service. As Andrew Carnegie once said, "No man can become rich himself unless he enriches others in so doing."

There are no exceptions to this law. If you want more money, then you must give more service to your customer or your client. That is the price you must pay to get what you want.

If you have not achieved your goal in the specific time period you've given yourself, it could well be that you have given yourself an unrealistic deadline. But I know you will have made progress, so the thing to do is simply to repeat your test, again and again if necessary. It will become so much a part of your life that you will wonder how you could ever have lived in the old way that you did.

Use this new way of life, this new system of giving yourself goals to attain, and eventually the flood gates of abundance will open and more riches will come your way than you ever dreamed possible. Money? Yes, lots of it, if that is your goal. But not only that, you will enjoy a calm, cheerful, successful, and happy life that few people even dream of.

A six-step program to help you become successful*

Here, now, I want to summarize in six easy steps how you can program your subconscious mind for successful achievement or self-improvement. This six-step program will show you how to program your subconscious mind with the right kind of input so you can gain the proper output from it.

---

*Based in part on the Million-Dollar Personal Success Plan of Paul J. Meyer, Chairman of the Board, SMI International, Inc., Waco, Texas. All rights reserved. Copyright 1962. Reprinted by permission.

1. *Set a definite goal for yourself.* Determine exactly what it is that you want to achieve. Then dedicate yourself to the attainment of that goal with unswerving singleness of purpose. Do not allow anything to interfere or get in the way.

2. *Develop a plan for achieving your goal* and give yourself a reasonable deadline for its attainment. Plan your progress carefully—day by day, month by month, year by year. A burning enthusiasm and perseverance will contribute to the achievement of your goal.

3. *Develop a deep and sincere desire* for the thing that you want. Remember that desire is the first law of gain. It is the greatest motivator of every action. The desire for success in your conscious mind plants a success-consciousness in your subconscious mind which thus creates an ever-increasing habit pattern of success.

4. *Never let the fear of failure enter your mind.* If you think for one moment that you will fail, then you will surely fail. But if you think you will succeed, then you most certainly will, for you'll be programming your subconscious mind with the proper thoughts. Just do the thing you fear to do and you'll gain the power to do it.

5. *Develop a supreme confidence in yourself* and in your own abilities. Concentrate on your strengths—not your weaknesses. You can change your self-image by writing out a description of the kind of person you want to be. Then you can act the part of that successful person you've decided to become. Believe that it is so, and it will be, for your subconscious mind will make it so.

6. *Be persistent . . . follow through.* Develop a sincere determination to follow through on your plan, no matter what obstacles you encounter. Here's the point where losers quit and give up, but winners never do. They keep right on plugging away. So be a winner. Don't quit. Never give up.

And now on to a most exciting and interesting chapter, *How to Deactivate and Defuse Your Failure Attitudes and Ideas* so you can become highly successful.

How to Deactivate and Defuse Your Failure Attitudes and Ideas

5

Strange as it might sound, 95 out of every 100 people fail to achieve anything of major importance in their lives simply because it is easier to fail or just coast along not living up to one's potential than it is to succeed.

Before we go any further in this chapter, I think I should give you my definition of success and failure. I have a feeling that our definitions of these two words might not be exactly the same.

To me, *success is the progressive realization of a worthwhile goal.* If a person is working toward a specific worthy goal that he has picked for himself, he is a success. A success is the person who is a plumber, mechanic, musician, salesman because that's the profession or occupation he really wanted to be in and he chose for himself. A success is also the housewife and mother who wanted to be a housewife and mother and who's doing an outstanding job of being one. In other words, the success is the person who is deliberately doing what he or she really wanted to do, not what someone else—a father or mother, for instance—wanted him or her to do.

A failure is someone who has the talent and the ability to accomplish much more than he has. If he has no predetermined goal, if he's just coasting along and not living up to his fullest potential, he is a failure, no matter what his position is or what his income might be.

Success requires strenuous effort, but it's a proven fact statistically that most people are as lazy as they dare to be and still get by. For instance, the failure does not have to work as hard, and he can avoid the struggle and pain of that strenuous effort by just taking it easy.

However, if you are an unwilling victim of that failure syndrome and you would like to make a change for the better, then this chapter will most certainly help you. When you use the techniques that I'll give you here,

YOU'LL GAIN THESE MAGNIFICENT BENEFITS FOR YOURSELF

1. When you deactivate and defuse your failure attitudes and ideas, you'll be able to channel your energy and your efforts in the right direction so you can become successful in everything that you do.

2. You'll learn to concentrate on worthwhile goals instead of frittering away your time on objectives of secondary or negligible importance.

3. Your self-esteem will increase and your self-confidence will soar as you discover you can succeed at whatever task you undertake to do.

4. Personal power, prestige, respect, and recognition from others will all be yours along with financial rewards when you rid yourself of failure attitudes and ideas and replace them with positive concepts of success.

Techniques You Can Use to Gain These Magnificent Benefits

How to deprogram your subconscious mind of its failure attitudes and ideas

As I told you previously, anything that is programmed into your subconscious mind will never be forgotten; it will always be retained for recall by your conscious mind when it is needed. This means, then, if you (or someone else) has been feeding failure ideas into your subconscious mind, you are going to get back negative ideas of fear and failure, for the output always equals the input. Or if you're just coasting along, taking it easy, unwilling to make the extra effort that's required for success, your subconscious mind will coast along, too. As I've said before, you must furnish the 98 percent perspiration that is necessary for success.

However, you can override these negative concepts that you have stored in your subconscious mind when you start programming it with success ideas instead of failure ideas. The moment you do that, your subconscious mind determines that your conscious mind is no longer interested in failure, so it buries these attitudes and ideas deeper and deeper into your memory banks. Even though those memories will always be retained, they will never surface again and enter your conscious mind *unless you allow them to do so.*

How, then, can you accomplish this important change? By following a very simple rule that is really the golden key to all successful achievement. Simply said, that rule is this:

ACT AS IF IT WERE IMPOSSIBLE TO FAIL.

That simple, short sentence is the formula that will allow you to make a complete about-face from being a failure to becoming an outstanding success. This does not mean you will not suffer some temporary defeats along the way; you no doubt will. But that does not mean you have lost the war; it only means you have lost one little battle. Every time you try a method that does not work, you will know to cross that one off your list and try again. Let me tell you about a man who practiced this technique of acting as if it were impossible to fail to the hilt to become highly successful in spite of numerous temporary defeats.

Joseph P. is president of an internationally known cosmetics firm that counts its annual receipts in millions of dollars. But it wasn't always that way. Less than 25 years ago, Joseph was fresh out of college with a sheepskin to prove that he had a degree in chemistry.

He was full of fire and enthusiasm to lick the world. Joseph wanted to come up with a foolproof formula that would keep cosmetics from deteriorating and spoiling. He had no idea of the odds against him in such a project. Even when warned by wholesale drug houses and cosmetic supply firms that he was tackling a job that even better men had failed at, Joseph nevertheless set out to do the job. He simply refused to accept the idea of failure.

"It took every cent I could spare from my job as a junior chemist with a petroleum refining company to buy laboratory equipment, chemicals, and ingredients for my cosmetics experiments," Joseph said. "I would mix a formula and put half in the refrigerator and half in the kitchen window in direct sunlight. I wanted a foolproof formula that would stand up in any kind of household temperature and any type of treatment.

"Well, nearly two years of hard work went by. One morning, somewhere in the 23rd month, I set my 179th experiment out—as usual, one part in the refrigerator and the other part in the kitchen window. And as I did, the thought came to me from somewhere deep inside, the prevention of mold and deterioration is not from some substance outside the cosmetic formula. The prevention of mold is within the mold itself and therefore—inside the ingredients of the cosmetic.

"From then on, it was all downhill. I don't know how many more experiments I made, but it didn't matter to me. I knew I had the answer. From that moment of revelation, it was almost as easy as picking up the parts of a picture puzzle that had fallen on the floor."

Joseph P. makes it all sound easy as he tells it today. But he succeeded where others would have given up and failed because he refused to accept temporary defeats as permanent failure. He continued to program his subconscious mind with the idea that it was impossible to fail so he eventually succeeded.

You, too, can do the same when you act as if it were impossible to fail and program your subconscious mind with that idea. That simple statement is the golden key that you can use to lock the door on failure and to open the door of successful achievement.

Let me point out to you here that it is extremely important to use the proper words in reprogramming your subconscious mind for success instead of failure. For instance, you should not say such things as "I am not a failure." That is not the way to program your subconscious mind for success. Failure is the only picture going into your subconscious mind when you use such negative words as *not, never,* and *failure.*

Negative words will not reprogram your subconscious mind even though you are trying to use them in a positive manner. Use positive words to program your subconscious mind. Instead of saying, "I am not a failure," say instead, "I am a success."

Don't let others program your subconscious mind with negative ideas

This is such an important subject for you to understand, I have divided it into four subheadings for discussion: (1) How others can program your subconscious mind, (2) How children can be improperly programmed, (3) How advertising people program your subconscious mind, (4) Don't accept negative advice from others.

1. *How Others Can Program Your Subconscious Mind.*

An important point to remember about your subconscious mind is that it will accept suggestions and take orders, not only from your own conscious mind, *but also from outside sources when your own conscious mind is bypassed,* if you allow that to happen. Let me show you now by a simple example exactly how this can work.

Let's suppose you're on a luxurious Caribbean cruise. You approach a fearful-looking passenger and say something like this: "You look very ill. Your face is terribly pale. You must be getting seasick. If you'd like, I'll help you to your cabin."

This person, who has been afraid all the time about getting seasick, now becomes extremely ill, all as a result of the negative suggestion you planted in his subconscious mind.

But if you were to make that same suggestion to a seasoned seagoing traveler or to a sailor, he would probably laugh at you. After many voyages, he knows he has nothing at all to worry about. Therefore, *his conscious mind rejects your negative suggestion and he does not allow it to enter his subconscious mind.*

Let me give you now a classic example of a person who knew how to play upon people's fears and program their subconscious minds successfully for his own benefit.

John Wesley, the founder of the Methodist faith, enjoyed an enormous success as an English evangelist. He had a shrewd and intuitive understanding of the inner workings of the conscious and subconscious minds.

He would open his sermon with a long and vivid description of the agonies and torture to which his listeners would be condemned for all eternity unless they became converted to the faith. Then, after a sense of terror, guilt, and extreme anxiety had brought his audience to the brink of a complete nervous breakdown, he would offer eternal salvation to those who accepted Christ and repented of their sins.

By this kind of "hell-fire and damnation" preaching, Wesley converted hundreds and thousands of people. Intense prolonged fear exhausted their nervous systems and produced a state of greatly intensified suggestibility. In this vulnerable condition, people accepted the preacher's theological message without question. They emerged from this religious ordeal with new behavior patterns firmly planted in their subconscious minds.

There are a few rare occasions when it could be an advantage to you to have your subconscious mind programmed by an outside source, but very, very few. Let me give you an example of one such:

Thelma's husband, Stanley, was a chain smoker of four packs of cigarettes a day. Thelma was greatly concerned for the health of her husband and rightly so. Each night as he sat in his easy chair in front of the television set half asleep, and again, after he had gone to bed, she would whisper softly in his ear several times, "Cigarettes cause lung cancer; stop smoking."

Several months passed and Thelma was about ready to give up this procedure when one day Stanley said to her, "I've decided to quit smoking." When she asked him why, he replied, "I don't really know why. It's just that something inside of me keeps saying not to smoke anymore, so I'm not going to." That was more than seven years ago and Stanley hasn't smoked a single cigarette since then.

2. *How Children Can Be Improperly Programmed.*

Children are especially susceptible to having their subconscious minds programmed by adults in authority. Parents and teachers are primarily responsible for doing this because of their relationships with children.

This is all part of a child's learning process and no harm is done as long as the programming is positive in nature. Unfortunately, much of the time the exact opposite is true.

If you are a parent, never, never tell your child that he is stupid or ignorant or dumb or that he will never amount to anything. I have a friend who to this day hates any sort of mathematics. Under hypnosis his hatred was traced back to a comment by a teacher who, when scolding him for a mistake, had said, "You'll never be any good at arithmetic."

My own nephew, who is in his mid-20s, to this day cannot add a simple column of figures or balance his checkbook without a calculator. His father used to make him drop his trousers and then whip him with the buckle end of a belt when he made a mistake in math. As a result, my nephew utterly despises arithmetic of any sort, and his subconscious mind refuses to have anything at all to do with figures.

If your son or daughter brings home a bad grade from school, just remember that your criticism can cause more harm than good. You can program a permanent inferiority complex into his or her subconscious mind. If your son flunks a math test, that doesn't mean that he's a mathematical failure. Or if your daughter fails one spelling test, that doesn't mean that she's illiterate or scholastically incapable. It just means that your children failed one test. That's all it means; nothing more.

I have learned over the years that praise is the best way to program another person's subconscious mind. So my wife and I have always gone out of our way to praise our children for whatever they've done. And we still do.

For instance, last Christmas, my wife said, "You know, our two grandsons have all sorts of trophies from Little League baseball, and their father has a bunch of golf trophies from tournaments, but Teresa doesn't have anything like that at all. Let's give her a big trophy for Christmas with the inscription, "The world's greatest female vocalist." And so we did.

If you're wondering about the inscription, perhaps you'll remember that I mentioned previously that our three children were all professional entertainers who perform together in a family group, *The Family Tree*. Our daughter, Teresa, is that group's female vocalist.

3. *How Advertising People Program Your Subconscious Mind.*

Fatigue increases your subconscious mind's susceptibility to suggestions or orders from a source outside of your own conscious mind.

Normally, your conscious mind acts like a guard at the gate. It filters out unwanted or negative information and keeps it from entering the storehouse of memory in your subconscious mind.

But when you're tired and worn-out, your conscious mind drops its watchful guard. It fails to fulfill its function of protecting your subconscious mind from outside suggestions and influences.

Commercial sponsors of television advertising know this full well. That is why they prefer the evening hours for plugging their products. Now if you were to ask them why, they would tell you because there are more television viewers in the evening.

Although that is true, it is not the major reason for their preference for advertising in the evening hours. They know that people are tired and worn-out in the evening and therefore more susceptible to suggestions from outside sources.

They also know that physical inertia favors mental relaxation and passivity, thus making the subconscious mind even more receptive to external suggestions. Since most of us spend our evening hours relaxing in a soft easy chair in front of the TV set, we are all perfect targets for the astute advertiser.

As one authority in the advertising business said, "During the day, a person's willpower resists with the greatest possible energy any attempt at being forced to succumb to another person's will. In the evening, however, when a person is fatigued, he will give in much more easily to suggestions from an outside source. That is why sponsors are perfectly willing to pay a higher price for nighttime television commercials."

From this you can see that you should never make a major expenditure, like buying a new car, for instance, when you're tired and worn-out. Take on that car salesman in the morning when you're fresh and alert and more capable of doing battle with him.

Smart merchants use more than the two physical senses of sight and hearing to sell their products. They also use the sense of smell successfully. A Minnesota sporting goods store increased its sales of fishing gear and camping equipment 20 percent simply by putting a fresh pine tree scent into its air conditioning system.

A New Jersey doughnut shop uses an exhaust fan to blow the aroma of freshly ground coffee beans and fresh doughnuts down on the persons passing in front of their place. You can imagine what happens when cold and hungry people walk by, especially on a blustery winter day in January or February. They've enlarged the shop three times and still it's standing room only.

The owner of an exclusive women's shop in California says this. "If two mink coats are modeled for a male customer and one model is wearing a seductive and sexy perfume while the other girl is not, he will almost always buy the mink the perfumed girl is wearing. Naturally, that mink is always much higher priced than the other one."

Sales to *men* in the ladies lingerie department went up over 30 percent in an Iowa store when suggestive perfumes were sprinkled along the counters and display cases.

If this small section on how advertisers go after your pocketbook by programming your subconscious mind will help you be on guard against them and save you money, then its place in this book is well-earned.

4. *Don't Accept Negative Advice from Others.*

You'll get all kinds of negative advice from people. You'll hear comments like these all the time: "It'll never work . . . you can't do it . . . that's impossible . . . don't waste your time trying it . . ." Don't listen to trash like this. Let it go in one ear and out the other, or better yet, plug both ears so you'll never hear it at all.

The world is full of pessimistic people who seem to love giving negative advice to others. For instance, not long ago I happened to see a book by about 40 prominent authors which was supposed to contain practical advice to aspiring writers. And even though I was not a beginning writer, I wanted to see what they said. However, most of their advice seemed to be that a beginning writer ought to take up some other profession to earn a living.

In fact, I got only about a third of the way through the book, for along about the 14th chapter, I read these words, "The odds against the beginning writer ever being published are about 50,000 to one!"

So I threw the book away. It was far too depressing to read, even for a published writer. I should have known better than to buy such a book, anyway, for a few years before that, I had bought a book entitled

One Hundred and One Don'ts for Writers. I had thrown that one away, too. I just don't see any sense in reading books that tell a person how to fail. That's programming your subconscious mind the wrong way.

You know, in this respect, I am often reminded of the aeronautical engineers who can prove to you by aerodynamics and the laws of physics that the bumblebee can't fly. You see, they say his wing span is far too small for the size and weight of his body, so scientifically speaking, it is impossible for the bumblebee to get off the ground and into the air. The trouble is, they forgot to tell the bumblebee that, so he goes merrily on his way to the consternation of all those brilliant scientists who say that it can't be done.

This example brings us full circle back to that golden key of success that I mentioned previously: *Act as if it were impossible to fail*. Do that and you can't help but succeed.

Don't place artificial limitations on yourself

You can place artificial limitations on yourself in many ways. One of the most common is to give yourself a goal that is far below your capabilities or to be too easily satisfied. Let me give you an example of that:

Henry Daley, a business management and sales consultant, told me this story from his own personal experience. Although the money mentioned in Henry's story has long ago been made obsolete by inflation, the principle involved still holds true today.

"I'd been called in as a sales consultant to a certain firm," Henry said. "The sales manager called my attention to a quite remarkable case. A certain salesman always managed to make almost exactly $10,000 each year, regardless of the territory assigned to him or the commission he was paid.

"Because this salesman had done well in a rather small territory, he was given a larger and better one. But the next year his commission amounted to almost the same amount as he had made in the smaller territory—$10,000.

"The following year the company increased the commission paid to all their salespeople, but this salesman still managed to make only $10,000. He was then assigned to one of the company's poorest sales territories—and again he made his usual $10,000.

"I had a talk with this salesman and found that the trouble was not in his assigned territory, but in his own evaluation of himself. He thought of himself as a $10,000-a-year-man, and as long as he held that concept of himself in his subconscious mind, outside conditions didn't seem to make much difference.

"When he was given a poor territory, he worked hard to make his $10,000. When he was assigned a good territory, he found all sorts of excuses to coast when the goal of $10,000 was in sight. Once, when the goal had been reached too early, he got sick and was unable to work any more that year, although doctors could find nothing physically wrong with him. Amazingly, he recovered completely by the first of the next year!"

As you can see from this example, this salesman set his sights far too low. He placed an artificial limitation on himself, and, in so doing, he sharply limited his capabilities and his earning capacity.

Never compare yourself with others

One of the quickest ways to program your subconscious mind with failure attitudes and ideas is to compare yourself with other people. When you do that, you are always going to meet someone who's better or smarter than you are in one way or another.

When you compare yourself with others, you'll be constantly programming your subconscious mind with negative thoughts like these: "She's more beautiful than I am . . . he's a lot smarter than I am . . . he makes more money than I do . . . " Such ideas lead to even more negative ideas like "I'm ugly . . . I'm dumb . . . I'm poor."

How can you stop this from happening? Easy. Just don't compare yourself with other people. Compete only with yourself. For example, if you are a salesperson, don't worry about being the top one in the company. Strive only to improve your previous performance by increasing your own sales. If you're on the company bowling team, don't worry about being the best bowler. Just work to improve your last week's bowling average. Do that, and sooner or later, you'll become the top salesperson, or the top bowler, or whatever you're trying to become.

Why nothing succeeds like success

Not only is programming your subconscious mind for success important in deactivating and defusing your failure ideas, but also an actual goal to reach is required. To reach a goal, action is necessary. You must do more than just think about it. You must actually do something.

I can well remember to this day—and that has been more than 40 years ago—when I went through the advanced infantry officers course at Fort Benning, Georgia. In our tactical exercises, we were faced time and again with the requirement to make rapid decisions.

As our instructors always told us, "Do something, even if it's wrong. Don't just stand there doing nothing. Remember that a poor plan carried out with vigor and enthusiasm can succeed where the best plan in the world which is never executed has absolutely no chance of success. Action of some sort is always required if you want to be successful."

So please remember this: If you are confronted with a problem, the longer you put it off, the bigger it becomes and the more fearful you are of your ability to solve it. Learn to trust your inner guidance from your subconscious mind. Make decisions and take action, for if you do not, you will invite total failure simply by your inaction.

You see, it's the fear of doing the wrong thing that paralyzes a person and attracts the wrong results. So make your decision and then act upon it. In so doing the chances are that your troubles will fade away into thin air—whether you make a mistake or not.

All great people are persons of quick decision which comes from their intuition, their accumulated knowledge, and past experience. So learn from them. Trust your inner guidance from your subconscious mind so you, too, can be quick in making your decisions and audacious in your actions. Act as if it were impossible to fail and you will always succeed. And nothing succeeds like success.

And now on to Chapter 6 where you'll see how you can use the powers of your subconscious mind to become a winner in everything that you do.

How to Use the Powers of Your Subconscious Mind to Become a Winner in Everything You Do

6

If you want to become a winner and succeed in everything you do, then you must constantly program your subconscious mind with positive and winning ideas. When you do that, its mighty powers will go to work for you to transform you into a winner.

I want to use this chapter to give you the techniques you can use to program your subconscious mind and feed it with positive and winning ideas and concepts. Then its output will equal its input and you can use its power to become a winner in everything you do.

Now then. Let me ask you this. What is it about successful people that gives them the winning edge? Why is it they never seem to lose? What is it that sets them apart from the crowd? Well, first of all, if you study winners carefully, you will discover that they have certain qualities that mark them as leaders and set them apart from the losers. Secondly, they always take winning for granted. They never once consider the possibility of defeat. In fact, they never allow themselves to even think about losing. To them, winning is a natural way of life. They believe wholeheartedly in Vince Lombardi's philosophy that *winning is everything; losing is nothing.*

With this attitude, a winner is able to be at home in any business or social environment. He can walk into any group and immediately become the center of attention. His manner and bearing instantly attract others to him.

When you learn to carry yourself like a winner, and act like one,

YOU'LL GAIN THESE FABULOUS BENEFITS FOR YOURSELF

1. You'll never run the risk of challenge to your position or your authority when you project the aura of a winner to others. People will respect you and have confidence in you. You'll gain their willing obedience, loyal cooperation, and full support.

2. You'll gain the reputation of being a "born leader." People will turn to you for answers to their problems. They'll trust you and ask you for your advice and help. When you act like a winner, you'll gain much power over others, for people will follow your lead without question.

3. You'll gain your own fair share of fame. You might not become president when you act like a winner, but you will become famous and well-known throughout your community, your city, or your state. Just how far you want that fame to spread is entirely up to you. The only limits to your success are those you place upon yourself.

4. You'll be transformed into a magnetic and powerful personality when you learn to act like a winner. You'll have an important new look, a masterful bearing, a new charm, a whole new status in life.

Do all these fabulous benefits sound like a miracle to you? I'm sure they do, but they can all come true when you know how to program your subconscious mind with the positive concepts and attitudes that you are a winner and not a loser. Take it from me and all those winners in life. Winning is everything . . losing is nothing.

The Techniques You Can Use to Gain These Fabulous Benefits

One of the most noticeable qualities in a winner is his charisma, which is often defined as *presence.* A winner literally radiates authority to those around him. He has the knack of assuming command of a situation, no matter what it is. When in his presence, people automatically defer to him and let him take over. Why is this so?

Because a winner is used to accepting full responsibility for his actions. His inner guidance from his subconscious mind lets him know that he is right in whatever he is doing. A winner immediately takes charge even when he lacks the authority to do so. And since most people do not care to accept responsibility, especially for a bad situation, they are only too glad to defer to someone who will take over the position of leadership. Let me give you an example of that.

How a winner reacted in a critical situation

An automobile accident had happened out in the country. Several cars had stopped, but no one had tried to help. Then another car stopped and the man who got out took charge of the situation immediately.

First he checked the occupants of both cars and found that the only person seriously hurt was a woman. Her face had been badly cut, one arm was broken, she was bleeding, and in shock. Since this was the dead of winter and the weather was icy-cold, shock was doubly dangerous.

This man checked to make sure she had no spinal injuries that would keep her from being moved. Then he turned and issued a series of rapid-fire orders to the people standing around.

"You there," he said. "Go in that house and call an ambulance. Then call the highway patrol. You over there, go with him. Bring back two blankets to cover this woman and a sheet or a towel or anything we can use to immobilize her broken arm.

"The two of you there, go and find something we can use to carry her into the house so we can get her out of this freezing weather. Get a folding cot, some boards, a door, anything at all that will support her weight.

"You two, go down the road to the south and slow traffic down. You two go up the road to the north and do the same thing. We don't want another accident here. The rest of you get in your cars and leave right now."

In only a few moments, where before there had been only confusion, there was now order and organization. All because one person had taken command of a bad situation. This man's manner and conduct were so positive and authoritative that no one questioned his orders or his right to give them. People jumped to obey his commands, for they were really anxious to help. They just needed someone to lead the way and assume responsibility for making the decisions.

That's the most important characteristic of a leader and it makes a person a winner every time. If you have the inner courage to make decisions and then to accept responsibility for your actions, you'll find that people will always acquiesce and let you take over the position of leadership.

You'll be surrounded by an aura of authority that, even though invisible, is still so easily recognizable a person can almost touch it. People will automatically regard you as a winner and look to you for leadership whenever a problem arises.

How a winner assumes control immediately

From the previous example, you can see that when two people meet for the first time, one will automatically become the leader and assume control of the situation. The other person will then become the follower. I'm sure you realize that winners are never followers; they are always the leaders.

You, too, can always seize control of the situation if you will simply remember that *everyone in the world is waiting for someone else to tell them what to do.* If you want to be a winner, then let that someone be you. You'll find that this strategy alone will single you out as the leader and the winner in any crowd.

All you need do is take the initiative and you will instantly have the momentum on your side. If you adopt a positive attitude and assume the other person is going to do what you want him to do, you'll find that 95 percent of the time, he will carry out your order or your command without hesitation or question. In 5 percent of cases, all he needs is a little extra push for motivation.

Why a winner is always optimistic and cheerful

Winners have learned to look on the bright side of things. They know that a smile speaks the universal language of love. It melts away resistance and opposition, quiets fears, inspires another person with hope and courage. Winners know that a sour-faced, pessimistic attitude is for losers, not for winners.

I can well remember a real winner by the name of "Happy" Weller whom I met back in the thirties when I was in high school in Sigourney, Iowa. Happy's nickname was well-earned. He was always cheerful and smiling. He had a good word for everybody. I never once saw him with a sour look or a frown on his face nor did I ever hear him say an unkind word about anyone.

Happy Weller was the owner and manager of the Keokuk Hotel, one of the most popular spots for miles around with traveling salesmen. They drove out of their way to stay at Hap's hotel. And because of his optimistic attitude and cheerful smile, Happy Weller became extremely successful and financially well-to-do as a result. He was a real winner and a positive example for others to follow.

Another aspect of the optimistic and cheerful winner is that he has learned not to take himself too seriously. He has developed a sense of humor that allows him to find the cheerful side of any situation.

A good friend of mine puts it this way: "I tried for many years to be successful," George says, "but I was never quite able to make the grade. So I finally decided that I must have the thing turned around somehow. So I decided to change my goals. I decided to become a failure and I was a success overnight!"

Of course, George is just joking. He's a success, an overwhelming success in the real estate business. He's just learned to keep his sense of humor, that's all.

How the winner gains respect from others

If you want to be a winner, if you want people to look up to you and respect you, then you must accept full responsibility for your actions, including your mistakes. When people know you are not going to pass the buck to them or blame them for your own mistakes, you'll gain their willing obedience, their loyal cooperation, and their complete and wholehearted respect and support.

Here are six simple guidelines you can use to program your subconscious mind properly so you can learn to accept responsibility, earn the respect of others, and be a real winner in their eyes.

1. Seize every opportunity that offers you increased responsibility. Don't wait to be told what to do; take the initiative and act on your own good judgment and inner guidance from your subconscious mind.

2. Do every job you've been given, large or small, to the best of your ability. I know that it's a cliché for me to say that any job worth doing at all is worth doing well, but it's still true, so I'll say it anyway.

3. Accept honest criticism and admit your mistakes. But don't indulge in self-pity. Move forward with complete confidence and courage.

4. Stick to what you think is morally right; have the courage of your own convictions.

5. Take full responsibility for the failures of those under you. This principle really determines whether you are a true winner . . . or just another loser.

6. Assume full responsibility for your own actions—for your failures as well as your successes. Most people are perfectly willing to accept the credit when things go right, but not the blame when things go wrong. But if you are going to be a winner, you must take the bitter with the sweet.

How winners handle their mistakes

I mentioned this point in the guidelines I just gave you for winning the respect of others. But it is such an important point it deserves some further amplification.

Mistakes are hard for the average person to handle. Criticism for those mistakes is even harder to take. Let me give you a for-instance:

Let's say you have people working for you and one of them asks you to check his work so you can show him what he's doing wrong. Now do you really think that's what he wants you to do? Of course not. He doesn't want you to criticize him and point out his errors. He wants you to praise him and tell him what a terrific job he's doing. I've yet to meet the person who asks for criticism and really means what he says.

If you are going to be a winner, you must know how to handle your mistakes with good grace. Even more important, you don't want those mistakes to be programmed into your subconscious mind and form a bad habit pattern.

So all you need do is recognize where you went wrong, admit your mistake to yourself, pick yourself up off the floor, and move forward with confidence and assurance. No recrimination or sense of guilt is necessary. It's about like getting bucked off a horse or falling off your bicycle. You simply get up, dust yourself off, and get right back in the saddle again. If you don't do that, you'll become paralyzed with fear of making the same mistake again.

Handled the right way, mistakes can help you. They build expertise. You'll know what doesn't work so you can then concentrate your efforts and energy on what does. A child learning to walk will fall down again and again, but as long as he gets up and tries again, he will eventually succeed. You are no different. You can handle your mistakes the same way a baby learning to walk does. The method is exactly the same.

Why a winner is always consistent in his actions

Winners are consistent in their actions. They say what they are going to do and then they do it. They make each commitment a personal matter and regard their word too highly not to follow through on what has been promised. If you want to develop consistency in your actions, then follow these six simple guidelines so you can program your subconscious mind with the right input.

1. *Practice absolute honesty and truthfulness at all times.* Don't allow yourself the luxury of even one tiny white lie. I can think of no exception to this rule whatever. Of course, this doesn't mean that you have to insult a person or hurt his feelings. If you can say nothing good about him, then do exactly that: say nothing.

2. *Be accurate and truthful in all your statements.* This includes statements both oral and written—official and unofficial. Your signature on any document, any report, any correspondence, or any piece of paper is your certification that the information it contains is correct.

By the same token, when you sign a personal check, your signature is your certificate that you have enough money in the bank to cover that check. Your signature in your work and on the job must carry the same weight.

3. *Stand for what you believe to be right.* Have the courage of your convictions. Never compromise your high moral standards; never prostitute your principles.

A great many times, one person's courageous stand can save the day. One man's courage and integrity in a situation where a tough decision is required can point the right way for an entire group.

Some time ago I attended a retirement function for a top-level executive of a large company in Orlando, Florida. The president of the company paid him his final tribute.

"Bob has been with our company for many years," he said. "In all that time, I have never seen him fail to stand up for what he believed to be right. Whenever a tough decision requiring integrity and courage had to be made, Bob always faced the issue squarely, no matter how unpleasant or unpopular his stand was. He always insisted that we make the right decision and he gave the rest of us the courage we needed to make it."

4. *Always keep your word.* To be consistent in your actions, you must be as good as your word and your word must be your bond. To make sure you always keep your word, remember and follow these three points:

a. Never make a promise you cannot keep. Some people do this simply to placate another individual or to get someone off their back, as it were, knowing full well at the time that the promise cannot be fulfilled.

b.   Never make a decision you cannot support. I have seen people in management and executive positions make wrong decisions so they would be popular with their subordinates. Yet when the chips were down, they would not support the decision that they had made.

c.   Never issue an order you can't enforce. I have also seen management people do this. They issue orders to please the boss, even though they know full well that their subordinates cannot carry out the order for it is impossible to do so. Then that same manager passes down the blame to his subordinates when the action ordered is not accomplished simply to get the monkey off his back.

If you don't keep your word, that makes you, to put it quite bluntly—a liar. If you are a liar, you are not consistent. You cannot be depended upon in any way; you cannot be relied on. You could be a genius, but as a leader, you'd be completely worthless. It is impossible for a liar to be a winner. I have given you few maxims in this book, but this is one of them.

5.   *Accept the blame when you are wrong.* This, too, requires you to be consistent. It also takes a high standard of personal integrity. Not only does a person have the tendency to pass the buck, but a great many times he will lie to get out from under.

Don't allow yourself to be caught in that trap. To lie trying to save your own skin and escape the blame only makes things worse. One lie leads to another and yet another, and you could soon find yourself entangled in a web of falsehoods. As I've already shown you, a liar cannot be trusted at all.

So the best thing to do when you are at fault is simply to accept the blame and get on to something else. When you goof, admit it. Don't look for someone else to be the scapegoat. After all, no one expects you to be perfect or infallible. Just admit it when you're wrong. People will gain confidence in you when you're consistently honest with them. You'll be a real winner in their eyes.

6.   *Don't carry your personal troubles to the office.* A friend of mine, a retired army sergeant, told me the finest person he ever worked for was a major.

"The major came to work every morning with a big smile on his face," Tony said. "He was always consistent. Not once did he come through the door with a sour look.

"When I retired from the army, I told the major he was the finest officer I'd ever worked for and that was the reason. He could always be depended upon to come to work with a cheerful and pleasant attitude which was a lot more than I could say about some officers I'd worked for.

"He told me he didn't believe in carrying his personal problems to the office or taking out his frustrations or anger on his men," Tony said. "The major also told me there were a lot of mornings he had to stand outside for a few minutes so he could crank that smile on his face before he came into the office. But he always managed to do so. He was the most consistent man I'd ever met and that made it a pleasure to work for him."

How a winner evaluates himself

Winners evaluate themselves on what they are, not on what other people think they should be. They do not allow themselves to be guided by other people's standards or beliefs. Winners do not allow others to act as their judge and jury.

Losers constantly worry about what they think other people are thinking about them. For instance, if your boss looks at you and frowns or if he sounds a little gruff in the morning, that's no reason to think he's angry with you.

He probably had a few cross words with his wife about the household bills before he came to work. Not everyone is able to crank a smile on his face as did that army major that Tony told us about a few moments ago. Your boss is probably one of those who isn't able to do so.

"I hear remarks like this every single Sunday," Reverend Charles Harmon told me. " 'We were in Orlando last weekend,' Mrs. Jones tells me. 'We went to church up there. I wouldn't want you to think we were over at the beach or something like that when we should've been here in church.'

"To tell you the truth, I didn't think that at all. In fact, I didn't even notice that she and her husband were absent until she called my attention to it."

I'll admit that years ago I, too, used to be concerned about what other people might think of me. Then I happened to see a movie in which the hero, an Easterner, had come west to marry his sweetheart, a girl born and raised on a Texas ranch.

One of the cowboys, the ranch foreman, made fun of the Easterner because of his city clothes and his city ways. He even challenged him to a fight, but the Easterner refused.

"Aren't you going to fight him?" his fiancée asked.

"Of course not," he replied. "It's not important."

"But what will people think of you?" she asked.

"I'm not responsible for what other people think of me," he answered. "I'm responsible only for what I think of myself."

Although I have forgotten the rest of that movie and I'm not sure whether the hero was Gary Cooper or Gregory Peck or someone else, I've never forgotten that one statement. It has helped me tremendously through the years in my relationships with other people.

You see, to worry and fret and stew about what other people might think about you is a complete waste of time. You never become what other people think of you. You become only what you think of yourself, and that, after all, is what really counts.

How you, too, can become a winner

You, too, have the ability and the potential to become a winner if you are willing to get rid of any negative concepts you might have of yourself as a loser. It is wise, of course, to recognize the past and to plan for the future by establishing goals for yourself. But if you allow the past and the future to fully occupy your mind, you will leave no room for the present.

Winners live in the ever-present now, keeping themselves busy with daily challenges and current goals to achieve. Dreamers live only in the future while losers get lost in the past, crying over missed opportunities, thinking to themselves, "If only I had done this . . . if only I'd been there . . . what if this had happened . . ."

When you focus your attention on the present, you can become completely responsive to it, aware of your present goals and what you have to do to reach them. If you find your mind wandering back to the past or straying forward to the future, bring it back to the present immediately. It is only through perseverance and self-discipline of your conscious mind that you can break your negative concepts and replace them by programming your subconscious mind with positive ones.

A positive concept of yourself and your own abilities to succeed are necessary to maintain a winning attitude. If you program your subconscious mind with a winning self-image, you can change the course of your entire life so it can become what you desire.

You are limited only by your imagination. As Albert Einstein, the renowned scientist, once said, "Imagination is everything; it is the preview of life's coming attractions."

So imagine yourself to be a winner. Program your subconscious mind with positive concepts and attitudes of love, success, and self-respect. As you think, so shall you become.

How to look like a winner

To have the look of a winner, so that people will give way to you on sight, you need not be 6 feet tall or built like a professional athlete. I have seen tall, strong men turn and run in battle while small, short men stayed and fought the enemy with courage. The power to be a winner comes from within, not from without.

Of course, there are certain physical characteristics you can develop to convey the feeling that you are a winner: a steady, unflinching gaze, a tone of voice that implies complete self-confidence, and, above all, a solid presence that lets people know you are exactly where you ought to be.

Your entire physical bearing is important in projecting the image of a winner. Your posture should be erect, your head held high, and your chest out. You should show alertness and vital energy in all your actions and movements.

If you have confidence in yourself and always act as if it were impossible to fail, people will gain strength from your example. Your appearance and manner then must depict confidence, sometimes even beyond what you actually feel. By controlling your voice and gestures, you can exert a firm and steadying influence over those around you.

People always have the highest regard for the person who remains calm in the face of trouble. And, conversely, they look down on the one who panics at the first sign of something gone wrong.

You increase people's confidence in you as a winner when you can view a bad situation with patience and a calm, cool presence of mind. By such a positive attitude, you seemingly take the burden all on your own shoulders. You give them the feeling that there is a way out of the dilemma and that the problem can be solved. People will have confidence in your strength, courage, and ability to make things right.

How to project the aura of a winner to others

When you see yourself as a winner and believe in your own abilities, an aura of self-confidence will literally radiate from you. It will be reflected in everything that you say and do. You'll glow all over with confidence and enthusiasm. And people are bound to accept you as a winner. They can't help themselves.

What makes a doctor, lawyer, businessman, or salesman a winner? Confidence in himself and enthusiasm for what he is doing. Let me give you an example of that:

Dr. J. is one of the finest clinicians in the state of Florida. He has served as Chairman of the Department of Internal Medicine at a famous Miami hospital for more than 15 years.

The hospital administrator told me that the moment Dr. J. enters the sick room, the patient begins to improve. "The art of healing seems to surround his physical body like an aura," she said. "It is often not his treatment but his physical presence that actually cures the patient!"

What better example of how confidence in yourself and in your own abilities can inspire others to have confidence in you and accept you as a winner is there than this?

If you, like Dr. J., can show by your every word and act that you are a winner and that you are confident of complete success, no matter how hard the job might be, you will inspire others to feel the same way.

Such self-confidence develops the habit of success, even the legend of infallibility. That's what really makes a winner.

And now on to a most informative and worthwhile chapter, *How to Program Your Subconscious Mind by Giving It Goals to Reach.*

How to Program Your Subconscious Mind by Giving It Goals to Reach

7

Your subconscious mind is a goal-seeking mechanism. If you will give it an objective or a target to aim for, then it will supply the means by which you can reach that goal. You do not need to concern yourself with the methods that your subconscious mind will use. If you will simply concentrate only on the goals you want to attain, the methods will take care of themselves.

But unless you give your subconscious mind a goal to reach, it cannot work for you. If you just coast or float along with no purpose or objective, then your subconscious mind will coast or float along, too.

In this chapter, I will show you how you can use goals for successful achievement. When you do that,

YOU'LL GAIN THESE VALUABLE BENEFITS FOR YOURSELF

1. The first big benefit you'll gain is successful achievement. That achievement may be financial success, improvement in your personal relationships with your family, your friends, and associates. It may be a more dynamic personality, improved health, or development of your inborn natural abilities. It all depends upon what goal you've given your subconscious mind to reach for you.

2. The second big benefit you'll gain with successful achievement of your goals is personal happiness. Life is too short to be unhappy. But you will never be truly happy until you are achieving a worthwhile and challenging goal. Your abilities are closely related to your desires. If you desire little, you will gain little, for you will not be required to exercise much of your true talents and abilities. One of the great leaders in the early Christian church, Augustine, said in effect, "Happiness comes from the attainment of the right desires."

Techniques You Can Use to Gain These Valuable Benefits

Why people without goals fail in life

I have read statistics that show that only five out of every 100 people become financially successful. By the retirement age of 65, only one of these people is truly wealthy. Four are financially independent. Of the remaining 95, five are still working, 26 have already died, and 54 are completely broke.

Now I know there are other ways of measuring successful achievement. I mentioned that in Chapter 5. But I also know that a certain amount of financial success is necessary for complete happiness. I have never been convinced that a person can come up with good ideas for successful achievement on an empty stomach. All he can think about is how hungry he is or how hungry or how cold his wife and his children are.

As Russell Conwell said in his magnificent little book, *Acres of Diamonds*, "Love is the grandest thing on God's earth, but fortunate is the lover who has plenty of money!" I couldn't agree more; that says it in a nutshell.

Why do these five out of every 100 succeed? Because of goals. They know where they want to go and they plan how to get there. Why do 95 out of every 100 fail financially? Because they have no goals to reach, no objectives to attain. They're like a ship leaving a port with no captain, no crew, no destination. They drift until they end up shipwrecked on the reefs and rocks of life.

If groups of people expect to succeed, then they must also establish goals to reach, just as individuals do. If they do not establish goals to attain, then they will fail, just as individuals do. For example, back in the 1930s a comparatively small religious movement built a large headquarters building in Independence, Missouri. It was called the Auditorium. The building seats thousands of people, it cost hundreds of thousands of dollars to build, and it was built primarily by small donations from its members right in the middle of the worst depression the United States has ever known. How was that possible? *Because the church gave its people a solid, concrete goal to achieve.*

But after the Auditorium was finished, the church began to stagnate. Today, it does not even retain its own natural increase. Why? Because when the Auditorium was finished, so were the people. They no longer had a specific and tangible goal they could shoot for. The church leadership failed to establish a new goal that its members could strive to reach. The Bible said it perfectly thousands of years ago: "Where there is no vision, the people perish." (Proverbs 29:18)

How you can use goals to increase the power of your subconscious mind

Just as an athlete must use his muscles to increase their strength, so must you use your subconscious mind to increase its power. The best way to do this is by giving it concrete goals to reach for you.

If you are at a loss as to what sort of goals to give your subconscious mind to gain for you, let me give you a headstart this way:

First, let's take *material possessions.* It could well be that one of these could be your goal: a good house, new furniture, a big automobile, a new wardrobe, a better job, promotion, advancement, financial security. All you need do to succeed is to make one or more of these your goal.

Or you might be more concerned with your *physical well-being.* Perhaps you'd like to have better health, a loss of weight, a better memory and concentration, the ability to relax and get rid of tension, rid yourself of certain undesirable habits—for example, smoking, excessive drinking, loss of temper. You can have whatever you desire if you establish a goal for yourself.

Perhaps you'd like to have *better relationships with people*: the admiration and respect of others, a position of authority and leadership in the community, the love of your family. Simply ask and believe that you have already received and you will.

Finally, there could be *spiritual goals* to consider. Perhaps you'd like a better and closer relationship with your Higher Power, the assurance of an inner serenity and peace of mind, freedom from past guilt, getting rid of fear, worry, and anxiety, the happiness of setting a worthy example for your children, your friends, and your associates. Whatever it is that you want, make that your goal, believe that you have received it, and it will be yours.

Three characteristics every goal should have

Every goal must have these three characteristics. If it is lacking in any one of them, it will usually be unobtainable for you.

1. *A goal must be concrete and specific.* You must know exactly what it is you want to attain. Just to say, "I want to be rich," is only wishful thinking. *How rich do you want to be?* If you want an income of $50,000 or $100,000 a year, then give that figure to your subconscious mind. Then leave it all up to your subconscious mind to furnish you with the ideas you need to make that deep desire of yours come true.

If your goal is not concrete and specific, you will find yourself in the same spot as that religious group who built the Auditorium that I told you about before. After it was completed, the church began to stagnate. It no longer grew or prospered because the leadership did not furnish the members with a visible, tangible, concrete, and specific goal to attain.

Intangible and nonspecific goals are impossible to visualize for they are too vague and abstract. They will not inspire or stir your subconscious mind to action for you. If you are not sure in your conscious mind of exactly what it is that you want, you are in no position to properly program your subconscious mind for successful achievement.

So if you want to reach your goal successfully, make sure that it is concrete and specific.

2. *Your goal must be measurable.* By that I mean you should be able to judge your progress toward the attainment of your goal. Your goal may be quantitative—how much you intend to do or how far you want to go.

For example, your goal may be to become president of the company you work for, no matter what your present position is. A certain man I know did exactly that. He rose from the mail room clerk to president of the company in just 16 years, for that was his goal.

Of course, he had to use some intermediate goals along the way to reach his final objective, but he never took his mind off his final goal, that of president of the company. He was determined to get it and he did. As he once told me, "The important thing to keep in mind is not where you were or where you are but where you're going."

3. *Your goal should have a definite time period.* When you draw up your plans to reach your goal, you should give yourself a definite and reasonable time period to attain your objective. If you do not do that, you'll find it is all too easy to procrastinate and put things off.

For instance, if you plan on becoming a doctor or a lawyer, you're not going to do that overnight. Or if you want to make a million dollars, you're going to need a definite time period in which to accomplish that.

So plan your progress carefully, year-by-year, month-by-month, day-by-day, even hour-by-hour if that becomes necessary. If you happen to miss one of the dates on your timetable, don't become discouraged and quit. You may need only to readjust your schedule. Perhaps you were a little unrealistic and too much in a hurry when you drew up your original timetable. It's more important that you are still moving in the right direction and in an unswerving line toward your goal.

Why it helps to get your goal down in writing

Before you force yourself to put down a specific goal on paper, it's all too easy to think in generalities, like this one, "I want to be rich by middle-age." But this is not a goal; it is only idle daydreaming or wishful thinking. A goal states how much you want in your savings account, for example, right down to the penny, by a certain and specific date; for instance, "I want to save $100,000 by my 35th birthday."

I'm sure you've heard someone say, "I know what I mean, but I just can't seem to put it into words." If you've ever been guilty of saying that, it means you're not completely sure at all of what you want or what you mean. If you can't get your goal down in writing, then you don't really have a specific and concrete goal yet with which to program your subconscious mind. You're still indulging in wishful thinking or idle daydreaming.

Let me give you a sample planning guide here to help you get started in getting your goals down on paper.

A 10-Year Planning Guide

1. *My profession:*

   a. What annual income am I shooting for?
   b. What level of management do I want to reach?
   c. How much responsibility am I willing to accept?
   d. How much authority do I want to command?
   e. What perquisites do I want in my position?

2. *My family:*

   a. What standard of living do I want for my family?
   b. What kind of house do I want for them?

   c. What part of town do I want to live in?
   d. Where do I want to take my family on our vacations?
   e. How much do I want to set aside for my children's higher education?

3. *My social life*:
   a. What kinds of friends do I want to have?
   b. What social groups or clubs do I want to become a member of?
   c. What community leadership positions do I want to hold?
   d. What worthwhile causes do I want to get involved in?

This is only a sample guide to help you get started so you can get your own goals down in writing. You can add or subtract items as you see fit depending upon your own particular situation, circumstances, and desires.

How to make your goal exciting and worthwhile

If you want to get out of the rut of boredom and complacency, then you must make your goal exciting and worthwhile. One of the best ways to do this is to visualize all the benefits you're going to gain when you reach your goal. Just for instance, let's say you want to stop smoking. Instead of trying to use willpower or thinking to yourself how difficult that's going to be, motivate yourself by listing all the good things that will happen to you when you quit. For example,

1. You'll no longer have that hacking smoker's cough.
2. Your food will taste better and smell better, too, for you will regain not only your sense of taste, but also your sense of smell.
3. You won't run the risk of offending others with halitosis for your breath will smell better. As my son, Bob, always says, "Kissing a girl who smokes is like licking out the bottom of an ashtray with your tongue."
4. You'll no longer run the risk of bronchitis, emphysema, or worst of all, lung cancer. It's a proven fact that your body begins to heal itself within only 12 hours of your last cigarette, although it will take several months before it ever returns to normal health.
5. You'll no longer run the risk of premature aging and facial wrinkles. It's also a proven scientific fact that women who smoke have more wrinkles at 50 than nonsmokers do at 70.
6. You'll save a small fortune in a year, enough to go on a luxurious vacation. A two-pack-a-day habit at $1 a pack costs you annually $730, and that's a lot of money, at least to me.

Now that's a carload of benefits you can gain when you reach your goal of not smoking anymore. And that makes your goal exciting and worthwhile. You can use the same sort of system of setting goals for losing weight, controlling your temper, making more money, whatever. The more exciting and worthwhile you make your goal, the more ambitious you will become to reach it and the better your subconscious mind will work for you.

Why you should never discuss your goals with anyone

I've touched on this point before, but I want to cover it in more detail here for it is such an important technique for you to use. To discuss your plans and your hopes with others can sometimes be extremely embarrassing to you. Let me give you an example with which I'm personally familiar.

In 1950, when the Korean War started, hundreds of thousands of reservists were directed to get a physical examination and be prepared to report for active duty within 30 days if they were in good health.

A friend of mine, an insurance agent, was ordered to report for his physical exam in July of 1950. Jerry was told that if he passed his physical he would be recalled to active duty within 30 days. He was found to be in perfect health, so Jerry closed his office, told everyone he was leaving for the service again, and soon found himself on the receiving end of numerous farewell parties and going-away gifts.

But as can so often happen with the government, there was a foul-up in the paperwork and his active duty orders did not arrive. Jerry waited through August, September, and October, and finally reopened his insurance office. It was not until February of 1951 that his paperwork was finally straightened out and he was recalled to active duty fully seven months after he had expected to leave.

You must also remember that everyone has different ideas about how to go about reaching a certain goal. If you were to ask 100 people, you'd get 100 different opinions as to what was the right way. So when you discuss your plans and goals with others, you are running the risk of total chaos and confusion in your mind. You alone are best qualified to know what you should do based on the information and guidance you receive from your subconscious mind. "Go and tell no man" is still excellent advice.

How to be a "one-eyed" man

Investment counselors will tell you to diversify so you will not run the risk of an investment in a single company going bad on you. That may be true for investments, but it does not apply here. To make your subconscious mind work at its maximum potential, give it only one goal at a time. Concentrate on a single point; don't scatter your fire.

That's exactly what Jesus meant when He said, "When thine eye is single, thy whole body also is full of light." So be a one-eyed man. Have a single purpose in mind that you want to achieve. Then you can exert all your efforts and energies on that one specific goal. As Andrew Carnegie, the steel magnate, once said, "Put all your eggs in one basket. Then watch that basket!" Concentrate only on one purpose at a time and you can become highly successful.

Why you should shoot for the moon

Don't be afraid to shoot for the moon when you establish your goal. You may have to use some intermediate goals as stepping-stones to your final one, but don't sell yourself short. Whatever you can imagine, you can achieve. Let me give you an example of someone who did exactly that:

At one time I was fortunate enough to visit the western part of North Carolina, better known as the *Land of the Sky*. But its green mountains, clear fresh lakes, clean running streams of water, and blue skies are not its only attractions. It also boasts of all kinds of textile mills, paper mills, plastic and rubber products factories, and many others. It abounds in industry, thanks mainly to its fresh, clear mountain streams.

A gentleman I met there, Jim Taylor, was the plant manager for the Waynesville, North Carolina, branch of a nationally known rubber company when I first met him. But less than two years before that, he'd been a shift supervisor in the same factory. How did he go up the ladder so fast in such a short time? Well, let's listen to what Jim has to say about that himself:

"I made my ultimate goal the plant manager's job," Jim says. "I prepared myself for it by always being ready to take over my boss's job. When I was a shift supervisor, I learned all the duties and responsibilities of my boss, the mill foreman. When he left the company to go to work for another outfit, of the three shift supervisors in the mill department, I was promoted to the foreman's job.

"During the time I was general foreman in the mill department, I made it my business to learn the main duties of the other general foremen in the plant.

"I wasn't trying to run the other fellow's business, but since my own department supplied everyone else with the raw materials needed to make their finished products, I had to know what was going on in their departments, too. Not only that, I knew that the next job up the ladder was that of the production superintendent, and to fill that position, I'd have to know the details of every job in the plant.

"That extra knowledge paid off for me, for during that time, more than once the plant manager and the production superintendent had to go up to Ohio together on company business. Of all the department foremen in the plant, Tom always picked me to run the plant in their absence.

"Well, about six months ago, Tom, our plant manager, got transferred to the main corporation offices up in Dayton. Harold, the production super, took over Tom's job and I became the production superintendent.

"But not long after that, Harold went to the midwest to take over our St. Louis plant and I got the plant manager's job here."

"What else did you do to prepare yourself for that manager's job, Jim?" I asked him. "I'm sure there was even more to it than just establishing a goal for yourself, wasn't there? I mean you had to prepare yourself for it, didn't you?"

"Well, as I say, I've always tried to know as much about the whole plant as I possibly could," Jim said. "I tried to learn all the details of my own job, my boss's job, and the jobs of each one of our employees.

"But I did even more than that, too. I'm not a college graduate, so I was taking some adult education courses at The University of North Carolina's Asheville campus on Wednesday nights and Saturday mornings. In fact, I still do.

"The company knew full well I was taking some college courses to improve my education, for they were paying half of my tuition costs. I guess they must have felt that continuing my formal education was important to them as well as to me. And it must have made a difference, for I was promoted ahead of others with much more seniority. I've always done the best I knew how so I could be ready to move up when the company was ready for me to do so. That has always been my objective."

Once you establish your goal and you know where you're going, then do as Jim Taylor did. Do everything you possibly can to achieve that goal. Don't let anything stand in your way. As I've said several times before, your subconscious mind will give you the 2 percent inspiration you need to succeed. But you have to give the 98 percent perspiration just as Jim did.

Incidentally, he is no longer the plant manager in the North Carolina plant. I received a letter from him just a few days ago. He is now in Ohio at the corporate headquarters as the vice-president in charge of all production throughout the entire United States. He now has nine plants to supervise instead of just one. I'm sure that before he's retired, he'll be the president and chief executive officer of the corporation. That's what goals did for him; they can also do the same for you.

How to make up your own plan for successful achievement

Over the years, I have read any number of plans made for successful achievement. But the best one I have ever seen was compiled by Paul J. Meyer, founder and Chairman of the Board of SMI International, Inc., of Waco, Texas. An expert in inspiring people to give it their best shot, Mr. Meyer calls his formula for success the . . .

Million-Dollar Personal Success Plan*

1. *Crystallize Your Thinking.* Determine what specific goal you want to achieve. Then dedicate yourself to its attainment with unswerving singleness of purpose, the trenchant zeal of a crusader.

2. *Develop a Plan for Achieving Your Goal and a Deadline for Its Attainment.* Plan your progress carefully, hour-by-hour, day-by-day, month-by-month. Organized activity and maintained enthusiasm are the well-springs of your power.

3. *Develop a Sincere Desire for the Things You Want in Life.* A burning desire is the greatest motivator of every human action. The desire for success implants "success consciousness," which, in turn, creates a vigorous and ever-increasing "habit of success."

4. *Develop Supreme Confidence in Yourself and Your Own Abilities.* Enter every activity without giving mental recognition to the possibility of defeat. Concentrate on your strengths, instead of your weaknesses . . . on your powers, instead of your problems.

5. *Develop a Dogged Determination to Follow Through on Your Plan.* Do this regardless of the obstacles, criticism, or circumstances, or what other people say, think, or do. Construct your determination with sustained effort, controlled attention, and concentrated energy. Opportunities never come to those who wait . . . they are captured by those who dare to attack.

A Summary of Highlights for You to Remember from This Chapter

1. Pinpoint your specific goal and dedicate yourself to its attainment. Set only one goal at a time—the one that is most meaningful to you at this particular moment of time.

---

*Reprinted by permission of Paul J. Meyer, Chairman of the Board, SMI International, Inc., Waco, Texas. All rights reserved. Copyright 1962.

2. Make a specific plan to reach your goal. Write down your goal along with your plan to reach it in simple, clear, concise, and concrete language.

3. Keep the payoff constantly in your mind. Think about it all the time. Build mental pictures of yourself achieving your goal. Use all your five senses to bring your total personality to bear upon it, if possible.

4. Drive your goal deep into your subconscious mind. Remember that your subconscious mind is fantastically creative. It never rests. Your subconscious mind will bring to fruition whatever desire or goal you have programmed into it.

5. Don't let thoughts of defeat or fear slow you down, or worse yet, stop you. Develop a fierce satisfaction and pride in your ability to surmount any difficulty. Your attitude should be one of "I will win!"

Now on to the next chapter which I know you will find most interesting and exciting, for its title is *How You Can Use the Power of Your Subconscious Mind to become Successful and Rich.*

How You Can Use
the Power of Your
Subconscious Mind to Become
Successful and Rich

8

I know I said before that success is the progressive realization of a worthwhile ideal. And so it is. I also know that a person can be successful without being wealthy. For example, some people, like ministers, priests, and educators, measure their success in spiritual or intellectual returns rather than financial. However, in this chapter I want to concentrate only on how to become rich financially.

Now I'd like you to look at the wording of the chapter title once more. Please note that the word *successful* precedes the word *rich*. I have a specific reason for saying it that way. You see, *success is not the result of making money; making money is the result of success.* Most people have this important law turned around. They believe that you are successful if you earn a lot of money. But the truth of the matter is that when you are highly successful, then you can earn a lot of money. So strive for success as your specific goal rather than money in your financial endeavors. Then money will follow as a simple matter of course.

Money is power and so you ought to be desirous of having as much of it as you can earn honestly. You can do more good with money than you can without it. One of the best ways to become rich is to enrich others. That's the philosophy that Andrew Carnegie, the steel magnate, used to make $500 million. He enriched others by lowering the price of steel from $160 a ton to $20 a ton and in so doing he benefited every person in America.

When you follow this principle of enriching others to enrich yourself,

YOU'LL GAIN THIS ONE HUGE BENEFIT

Money, money, and more money. Ever since the Phoenicians invented money several thousand years ago, the primary aim of almost every person has been to accumulate as much of it as possible. This chapter will give you the techniques you can use to do exactly that.

How to Conquer the Poverty Complex

Before I take up the techniques you can use to become successful and rich, I first want to tell you how to rid yourself of the poverty complex if you have one, and many people do. Then we can start off fresh with a clean slate of positive ideas after getting rid of this negative one.

You see, a great many people are handicapped by having a poverty complex. This alone can prevent financial success. I knew a very capable young doctor of chiropractic, Kelly C., who was struggling to make ends meet. The roots of his problem lay deep in his own childhood.

Kelly's parents had been dirt-poor. There'd been many times when there wasn't even enough food in the house to eat and Kelly had often gone to bed hungry. He wore patched, hand-me-down clothes and did odd jobs after school to help supplement the family income. Whenever Kelly wanted something, the answer was always the same: "We can't afford it; we don't have the money; we're too poor."

Kelly was determined to get ahead in life and with the help of a chiropractor, a scholarship, and working part time he was able to get his degree as a doctor of chiropractic and start his own practice.

But Kelly was still thinking in terms of his childhood. He charged only a pittance for his services for he always felt that people couldn't afford to pay even a reasonable fee. Finally I was able to convince Kelly that just because he'd been raised in poverty that didn't mean that all his patients were poverty-stricken, too.

Kelly finally realized that I was right and that his low fees were entirely out of line with what his services were actually worth. He raised them considerably after he rid himself of his poverty complex that had plagued him since childhood. His income increased greatly when he learned to reprogram his subconscious mind with the proper success concepts.

If you have been bothered with a poverty complex yourself that's a hangover from your childhood just as Kelly's was, remember that if your parents were poor, that does not mean that you have to be poor, too. Reprogram your subconscious mind with ideas of material success, learn to evaluate your services properly just as Kelly did, and you can become financially independent yourself.

FIVE TECHNIQUES YOU CAN USE TO PREPARE YOURSELF FOR GAINING FINANCIAL SUCCESS

1. *Use Your God-Given Talents to Do What You Were Meant to Do.*
How is it that one person can be a top-notch salesperson and 99 others can be complete duds? What makes some musicians and singers the best in their field? Why do some lawyers turn away clients while others chase ambulances? How do some doctors get their patients well while others couldn't treat a mosquito bite? Why is one person a brilliant success and 100 others abject failures? What makes the difference anyway?

The successful person is successful because he is using his God-given talents to do what he was meant to do . . . what he is best fitted by his natural abilities to do. He is doing what he can do best of all. I am not implying that fate or destiny controls your future. Not at all. I am simply saying that it is absolutely impossible for you to become the greatest in your chosen field and be highly successful unless you are in the right profession to begin with. You must be doing work that will utilize your best talents to the fullest. How can you become completely successful unless you're doing what you really want to do, unless you're doing what you're best fitted by your natural talents to do?

Fortunate indeed is the person who goes to work with a smile on his face each day because he loves his job. Fortunate is that person who goes to work happy because he really wants to go to work, not just because he has to earn a living. The person who doesn't love his job isn't doing what God meant him to do with his talents. He's traveling through life third-class when he could have gone first-class all the way. He'll never reach the top and become highly successful and wealthy doing a job that he hates.

Let me sum up this idea by saying that one of the most important steps you can ever take in your entire life is to find out what you're best suited for in the first place. And the earlier in your life that you find that out, the better off you will be. Don't try to make yourself into something for which you have no inborn talents.

If you don't have the physical attributes to become a professional football player, then don't try to become one. Or don't allow your subconscious mind to be programmed by your parents so that you think you have the abilities and the desire for a profession you basically don't care for at all. Parents are often guilty of trying to make their children into what they wanted to be but were never able to become.

Don't settle for something that's second or third best. Once you know what you're best fitted by your natural talents to do, then go for broke; go all the way. Pull out all the stops. You know you will never be completely happy doing a job that you don't like to do and one that you're not fitted for. So use your God-given talents to do what you were meant to do. You can become highly successful and financially independent when you do.

2. *Accept Your Limitations with Good Grace.*

Accepting your limitations with good grace is just as important as developing your God-given talents. Every man who is five foot six, nearsighted, baldheaded, and overweight wants to look like Burt Reynolds, Tom Selleck, or whoever the current movie idol is. But no amount of wishful thinking can turn the trick for him. We can't all be movie or TV stars, professional football and basketball players, or homerun hitters.

When I was in high school I wanted to earn a letter in football in the worst way. But I never tipped the scales at more than 118 pounds soaking wet back then. So after three cracked ribs, one bent nose, two missing teeth, and a badly twisted knee, I finally accepted my physical limitations and gave it all up as a bad job. One of the best moves I ever made!

"When you learn to accept your limitations with good grace, then you can begin to use your real talents," says David Young, a nuclear physicist at a famous California university. "When I was a small boy I lived on a farm here in California. I loved the outdoors, and I spent every minute that I could exploring the wonders of nature in the hills that surrounded our fertile valley.

"One afternoon I was walking along the top of a high ridge when I spotted a hawk in a tall tree that leaned way out to overlook our farm. I saw a nest in that tree, and I felt sure that there must be some eggs in that nest. I wanted those eggs so badly so I could take them home with me to hatch, but I knew it was impossible for me to reach that nest without breaking the tree limb and falling down the mountainside.

"So I closed my eyes and I prayed. I prayed to God to let me fly up to that nest just like the hawk so I could get those eggs. And as I prayed, I thought I ought to show God I had some faith, too, so I flapped my arms up and down as fast as I could just like a bird's wings. I was so sure that God would hear my prayer and answer it, but, of course, nothing happened.

"And then the hawk flew into the air so gracefully from the nest. I was so envious. But as it flew away, a feeling of understanding came to me, young though I was, that God could not interrupt or change the orderliness of His creation just so one little boy might fly.

"From then on I think I knew deep down inside of me, that to be truly happy, one had to follow his inner guidance so that he might do what God had given him the talent to do. And that a person should also accept the limitations that had been placed upon him as exactly that—limitations—and nothing more. Only then could a person realize his true potential, do great things, and fulfill his own individual destiny."

I, too, over the years have learned to accept my limitations. For instance, I cannot sing. I have a voice that would frighten a bullfrog into silence. Nor could I have been a carpenter or a cabinet maker. I am so clumsy with tools that if I so much as pick up a hammer, my wife heads for the back bedroom, shuts the door, and covers her ears.

Some years ago I ran across a small verse which has been credited to Saint Francis of Assisi, although I think it has been rephrased by other wise men down through the years. It has helped me tremendously in accepting my own limitations. I feel sure it will help you, too. It goes like this:

> God grant me the serenity to accept
> the things I cannot change,
> Courage to change the things I can,
> And wisdom to know the difference.

3. *Acquire All the Specialized Knowledge You Can About Your Chosen Field.*

Now you may have all the natural ability that it takes to become a top-notch doctor or lawyer, engineer or chemist, businessman or company executive, but that won't be nearly enough. Especially in today's highly technical, scientific, and computerized world you will need specialized knowledge.

"Knowledge is that acquired information which includes both your professional learning and your understanding of people and what they want," says Roberta Wilson, a chemical engineer with a large nationally known company. "Nothing will inspire people's confidence and respect in you more quickly than your demonstration of that knowledge and your ability to put it to work to get results. You cannot conceal a lack of knowledge about your job. You cannot bluff people about that, at least for very long."

Remember that a degree is only the first step in the continual process of acquiring specialized knowledge about your chosen field. Continue to study, read, and to research into every corner of your profession. Sharpen those talents God gave you. Improve them every chance you get. The more you know about your work, the better your chances are of getting ahead and becoming highly successful.

4. *How to Become the Authority and Expert in Your Own Field.*

The only way to become the authority and expert in your own field is to *know your business and keep on knowing it.* By that I mean you must keep up with all the latest developments in your field. For instance, a certain physician I know, Dr. Anna S., a specialist in rheumatism and arthritis, is 69 years old. Yet she still spends four to six weeks every year attending lectures and seminars to keep herself up-to-date with the latest developments in her profession. Is it any wonder that she is regarded as one of the country's top experts in her field?

So if you want to be the authority and expert in your own field, no matter what it is, you'll want to do the same. Never stop studying. You'll never live long enough to know everything there is to know about your profession.

Not only must you retain what you have already learned, but you must also keep current with new techniques and procedures so you can be ready for the future. No matter what you do, you'll need to keep on learning for each new day brings about change of some sort.

To retain your position as an authority and an expert in your own field, continue your professional education and development. There simply is no other way.

5. *Develop Your Own Self-Image of a Successful Person.*

It is highly important that you establish your own self-image. You can do nothing that is in conflict with your own image of what you really are. For instance, it is absolutely impossible for you to become the greatest in your own field if deep down inside you don't really believe that you are the greatest.

Your actions, your feelings, your behavior will all be consistent with the image you have of yourself. In other words, you will act like the sort of person you conceive yourself to be. Not only that, you really could not act in any other way, in spite of any conscious effort or use of willpower on your part.

That is why it is so terribly important that you create a successful self-image. Your self-image should not copy or emulate another person to the point that you submerge your own personality in his. That is why the first two steps, *using your God-given talents to do what you were meant to do* and *accepting your limitations with good grace* are so vital in establishing your own proper self-image. They allow you to become the *real you* when you use them as guidelines.

You see, you cannot copy someone else successfully simply because there is no other person on this earth who is exactly like you. Just as fingerprints differ, so do physiques and personalities. You are a specific and unique individual. You will never come this way again. You are not like any other person on this earth and no other person is precisely like you. There is only one original; God doesn't make any carbon copies.

And that is why you can develop your own self-image by using your God-given talents as they were meant to be used and by accepting your limitations, not as defects or imperfections, but exactly as they are, limitations, that and nothing more. People are a very special and individual proposition. They do not come off the assembly line like Fords, Chevrolets, and Plymouths.

The Magic Formula That Leads to Financial Success

The magic formula for financial success has never changed since the first coins were minted in Asia Minor. It is six simple words: *Find a need and fill it.* Now let me show you how to use that magic formula so you can become successful and rich.

The key to this is to first use your thinking mind to find out what people need. Once you've found that need, then turn everything over to your subconscious mind to get the answer of how best you can fill that need for them. Let me give you an example now of someone who did that and how he became highly successful and rich in so doing.

Guy Fowler was an Iowa farmer back in the days when horses were used by most farmers instead of tractors. And fathers always looked forward to their wives having sons to help them on the farm.

In Guy's case, the first child born was a daughter. "Maybe the next child will be a son," Guy said. But the next child born was another daughter. And then came the final blow. The third time there were twin daughters!

So Guy gave up. "I can't run a farm with four daughters and no sons," he said. He sold the farm and moved to town.

"What are you going to do for a living?" his wife asked. "You don't know anything but farming."

"I don't know yet," Guy said, "but I'll find something to do where I can use my four daughters to help me."

As it happened, the first place they lived in had a tiny kitchen that was almost too small to prepare a meal for six people, so they ate out as often as they could afford to. But, unfortunately, there wasn't a decent restaurant in the entire town in which to eat.

After a month of this, Guy got up one morning and said to his wife, "I know what we're going to do for a living. There is a real need in this town for a good restaurant. We're going to open one. You're the best cook I've ever known and we have four daughters who can be waitresses."

"Are you sure that you know what you're doing?" his wife asked. "You have no experience whatever in the restaurant business."

"I'm sure," Guy replied. "I've thought about this for several nights now. I've prayed about it, too, and this morning when I woke up, it was as if a voice had spoken to me during the night in a dream. The voice told me to open a restaurant here for there was a great need for one. You know that's true as well as I do, for this town simply does not have a good place to eat. There isn't a good restaurant anywhere."

And so Guy followed the inner guidance he had received from his subconscious mind, even though he didn't know that he had one and he didn't know where his hunch of what to do for a living had really come from. He only knew that the feeling was there.

Guy ran one of the most successful restaurants in north central Iowa for 25 years. Salesmen went out of their way to stay all night in the town so they could eat at the Supermaid Cafe. On Sundays he served only fried chicken and there was always a long line of people waiting to get in to be served.

And each of his four daughters worked in the restaurant while they lived at home before they moved away to establish their own homes and raise their own families. I'm very familiar with Guy Fowler's restaurant and his success story. You see, I married one of his twin daughters.

SIX TECHNIQUES YOU CAN USE TO FILL PEOPLE'S NEEDS

As I told you a few moments ago, the magic formula that leads to financial success is to *find a need and fill it*. The next six techniques will show you exactly how to do that.

1. *How to Make Yourself Valuable to Your Company.*

I know that no one is indispensable, but you can make yourself so valuable to your company that your boss will think that he can't possibly get along without you. Knowing your job inside-out is one of the best ways of making yourself needed by your boss. Even if you have serious personality flaws, they can be overlooked as long as you can do your job better than anyone else can do it. You might even be thought of as a nonconformist and a queer duck in some ways, but just as long as you are really needed and wanted, no problem.

It's comparatively easy to get a position today; keeping it, however, is another matter. Once you go to work, it's up to you to prove that you can really handle your job. You know that your boss will follow up on your activities to see how you're doing until he's well-satisfied that you can handle things on your own.

So become an expert in your own specific field. Be willing to share your knowledge with others and your reputation for being needed will grow and grow. People will look to you for the answers. And that's good; it enhances the positive image your boss has of you.

Remember that if you are really good, there is no limit as to how far you can go. First of all, not every clerk wants to become an executive. Not every draftsman wants to become an engineer. Some salespeople don't want to become a sales manager. Many a sergeant has turned down an officer's commission in the service.

A lot of people are perfectly content with the jobs they have and where they are right now. And that's perfectly all right if that's what they want. But I assume you want something more for yourself. Otherwise you wouldn't be reading this book. And no matter what you are doing right now, I know you can be happier by doing your job better, earning recognition for doing it, and by preparing yourself for promotion and advancement.

How can you best make yourself needed by your boss? Well, to give you an example, let's pretend for a moment that you are a salesperson. The best way you can follow through on your job is to increase your knowledge of your own product and the products of your company's competitors. You should acquaint yourself thoroughly with company policy; the history of the industry; the whole manufacturing process of your product from beginning to end; your company's research and development program; its marketing operations; your own customers' peculiar and individual problems. Do these things and you'll be able to answer any possible question about your company and your product. And in so doing you will make yourself more valuable to your company. You will make yourself needed and wanted by both your boss and your customers by following through and learning everything there is to know about your job.

2. *Gain a Reputation for Being Dependable.*

Once you know your job thoroughly, your next step should be to make it well-known to the right people that you can always be depended upon to do that job and do it well. About the finest reputation you can build with your superior is to have it said of you that "you get things done."

If you are going to earn that reputation with your boss, he must be able to rely upon you to carry out his orders actively, aggressively, intelligently, and willingly. Do not misunderstand me here. Your boss should not expect blind obedience from you. Dependability does not demand that. A reasonable boss will always be willing to listen to suggestions for improvement from his subordinates. If he is not willing to do that, then I'll wager you'll soon be his superior.

Here are six specific steps you can take to develop the quality of dependability. They are:

1. Never make excuses for failure.
2. Don't evade responsibility by passing the buck.
3. Do every job to the best of your ability, no matter what your personal feelings are about it.
4. Be exact and meticulous about doing the details of your job.
5. Form the habit of always being on time.
6. Carry out the intent and the spirit as well as the literal meaning of the order.

3. *Why You Should Make the Extra Effort.*

The person who earns $100,000 a year is not five times as smart as the one who earns $20,000 a year. Far from it. In fact, he's probably just a tiny bit smarter. A little increase in knowledge can bring about a tremendous increase in salary. The $100,000-a-year man has to be only a little bit better than the other fellow. All he needs is the slightest edge and he usually gets that edge by making the extra effort that it takes to win.

Look at Sears Roebuck, for instance. At the end of 1964 they held the number-two spot for total volume of retail sales. They were the second largest retailer in all the world. The Great Atlantic and Pacific Tea Company was the biggest. But Sears was not satisfied to hold down second place. They wanted to be the biggest retailer in the world and by the end of 1965, they were number one, and they still are. How did they reach that number-one spot?

They used many procedures, of course, but here are just a few of the main ones. One of the most dependable is the method of selling all the extras along with the main item, for example the socks, shoes, tie, and shirt to go along with the suit.

Another highly effective method is that of guaranteeing satisfaction or your money back—no time limit—without ever a single argument or question. Still another is the motto of "No money down" on anything you buy at Sears. They also have the best customer follow-up in the business. When they say, "Sears services what it sells," they meant just that—they do.

Sears has also learned the art of telephone selling. My wife answers the phone at least once a week to find them on the other end of the line calling her attention to some special sale or bargain to be had in their store. Although courteous to the core, Sears is still the most aggressive telephone seller in the world. And they never give up. They always make the extra effort.

Sears also makes the extra effort to get every single employee of theirs to go all-out to render service to the customer. They know that the average person will form his judgment of the entire company through his contact with only one individual. If this one person is rude or inefficient, it will take a lot of kindness and efficiency to overcome this one bad impression. Sears knows that every member of their organization who, in any capacity, comes in contact with the public is a salesperson and the impression he makes is an advertisement, either good or bad. The person who makes a bad one won't be with Sears for very long.

So if you have ever wondered how Sears got to be as big as it is, now you know. They make the extra effort it takes to get that way. You can do the same thing, too. Just shift yourself into overdrive and follow through. Only one or two out of every 100 will make that extra effort it takes to go clear to the top of the financial heap. No reason why it shouldn't be you.

4. *If You Want to Get More, You'll Have to Give More.*

If you want to get more, then you'll have to give more—and the more that you give, the more that you'll get. You'll have to go the extra mile. In these United States, anyone can earn a living without going that extra mile. But if you want the economic security and the luxuries available in this country, you'll need to practice this technique and live by its philosophy until it becomes an ingrained part of you.

Let me tell you now about an ordinary, everyday fellow who goes that extra mile and how he benefits by so doing. I think you'll be doubly surprised to discover that he's a car salesman when you consider the low regard that most of us have for politicians and car salesmen. But I can assure you that this man is completely different from any of those you've ever met before. But I'll let him tell you about that himself:

"You don't go into the car business—you grow into it," says George Phillips, a 72-year-old salesman with a midwestern Ford agency. "When the average car salesman sells a car, he hurries to get the buyer out of his sight. Maybe he's ashamed of the deal he's just made, but he acts like he never wants to see or hear from that customer again. Mister, that kind of a salesman is a flop. He floats from one car agency to another, and eventually leaves the car business altogether. And the sooner he leaves—the better!

"If there is a single clue to success in the car business, I'd say it can be found in these words: Go the extra mile! I have a card file of customers that goes back for more than 40 years. Because of my friendship with their parents, I have a lot of names of sons and daughters in my customer files, now even the names of some grandsons and granddaughters! But I wouldn't have all those names if I hadn't followed up, gone the extra mile, and kept track of every single one of them.

"When a man buys a car from me, I make it a point to turn him into a close personal friend. I call him in a couple of days, then in a week or so, and even a month later to see if he has any question about his new car's operation, or if he's had any problem with it. *I don't wait for him to call me; I call him first.* If I wait until he calls, I know he's got a problem and then he's usually mad about it.

"I always talk to him every time he comes in to have his car serviced. On his first visit I take him back and introduce him to the service manager. I spend a few minutes with him every time he comes in to build up his confidence and trust in me.

"I want to make sure that he remembers who I am. I'll bet you anything that if you talk to any ten people you meet on the street today, even in a small town, seven of them won't remember the name of the salesman who sold them their last car. Why? Well, he's never talked to them again, that's why. In fact, he's probably avoided them completely.

"But I don't want my customers to forget my name. I want to make sure that they remember me. After all, the average person will buy from ten to 15 cars in his lifetime. I want him to buy them all from me!

"So I make him hungry for more information. Men love to talk shop about cars, their mechanical operation—engines, horse power, gas mileage, and so on. But so few of them really know enough about a car to discuss it intelligently. And a lot of so-called salesmen don't know how either. They don't know what's under the hood of their own product.

"I use that year or two between this new car and his next one to fill him up with facts about engine design and operation. That way he'll understand the engine improvements I'm talking about when the next model comes out. I give him tips on how to check minor mechanical points himself; how to cut down on tire wear; how to increase the life of his battery; and anything else new that comes along.

"When his new car is two years old, I contact him when the new models come out. I don't just send him a piece of advertising literature with my name rubber stamped on it. Any old car salesman can do that.

"I've worked up a small brochure to give him some facts and figures about his old car and the new models. I mention all the new designs, new features, accessories, and so on. I tell him all the advantages he will enjoy with this new car. I make him hungry for a new model.

"By now he has real confidence in me. He looks upon me as an old and trusted friend. And take it from me, people are real touchy about dealing with just any salesman when they're buying a new car. They're absolutely scared to death of a stranger, and I'm glad of that, for you see—I'm no longer a stranger.

"I resell 85 percent of my old customers. My repeat business is really amazing. But I get it simply by giving just a little bit more than other salesmen do and as a result, I get a whole lot more in return."

You might ask why George is still selling cars when he's 72. The answer is simple. He loves the work he does for he feels he's really helping people, and I know that he is. He could have retired years ago, but he just doesn't want to.

As you can see, George has benefited by making more money for himself than the average car salesman does. He has insured continued success for himself by giving more to get more. He has also gained a lot of secondary benefits besides money from his profession. He has gained a lot of friends who respect him, trust him, and who have confidence in his judgment and ability. When you learn to give more to get more, you can expect the same kind of results and benefits that George has received.

5. *How to Give Them More than the Other Fellow.*

This is another way to insure success for yourself. Let me give you an example. In Ames, Iowa, there is a little store known as *The Cookie Lady's Shop*. The owner of this busy establishment, Mrs. Baylor, is better known throughout this bustling college town as "The Cookie Lady."

"How is it your place is always packed with customers when your competitor's store across the street is almost empty?" I asked Mrs. Baylor.

"Oh, that's an easy question to answer," she said with a smile. "I always make sure to give my customers more than he does. First of all, I give everybody a baker's dozen—13 for the price of 12. Grown-ups get a free cup of coffee while they're waiting for me to sack up their orders. And that really brings a lot of people in here from October to April. We get some mighty cold winters here in Iowa.

"Little girls rate a kiss and a pat on the head along with a couple of my special sugar cookies; little boys get the same treatment except that I shake hands with them. Makes 'em feel like grown-ups. And everyone, big or small, young or old, rates a cheerful smile and a sincere 'Thanks a million!' for coming in my store.

"That fellow across the street is interested only in making a sale. I'm interested in gaining a permanent customer. That's why I always give them more than he does. That way I know they'll be back for sure. Why, some of my little sugar cookie customers have grown up on me, but they still keep coming back for more since I always give them more than the other fellow."

Now Mrs. Baylor well understands people, human nature, and the secret of financial success. She knows that if two storekeepers are offering people the same thing, then the one who gives them more than the other one does will keep them coming back to his store.

So that is exactly what she does. She always gives them more than the other fellow. It's one of the best ways in the world of making sure that customer keeps coming back to you for more. That's the secret of this technique. Simple, but highly effective. Just give them more than the other fellow does.

Remember always that the object of a person in business should not be to make just a single sale, but to make a permanent customer. In every business, it's a maxim that the first sale is always the hardest. It's like getting the first olive out of the bottle or a girl's first kiss. After the first one—the rest will come quite easily. It is also true that after you've made your first sale, your hardest work will be over. Your real profits will start when that person becomes a regular customer of yours and when he keeps coming back to you for more.

6. *How to Give Them More than They Pay For.*

This is the last of the six techniques you can use to fill a person's need. There is only one place I can think of where this technique will not work. It does not apply on Sunday mornings when the preacher's sermon runs overtime. This is one time no one wants to get more than he pays for. But other than that, there is no exception to this simple rule. Let me give you an example of this technique:

I know that today with supermarkets everywhere, the small individual meat market is slowly disappearing. But I know of one that is still highly successful and I am sure it will remain that way.

Mervin McClenahan is one of the few remaining independent butchers in the country who still makes an excellent living by specializing only in select cuts of meat. And what with all the serve-yourself meat departments in the supermarkets, individual meat markets where you can pick out the exact steak or roast or chops that you want are becoming as rare as the blacksmith shop and the harness store.

But Mervin still earns a good income in his small, but highly successful, market. "How do you manage to do it?" I asked him. "Especially when you sell nothing but meat?"

"I give them 20 ounces to every pound," Mervin says. "Sure, those supermarkets sell meat cheaper than I do. They ought to; they buy cheaper meat! But they can't give you the personal service that I can. Besides, they weigh the paper, too. And you get to see only one side of your meat. They hide the other side with that cardboard.

"But I give every customer of mine the extra special touch Everyone who comes in here is a VIP. A lot of my men customers like to come back in my big walk-in freezer and show me the exact porterhouse they want and how thick they want me to cut it.

"My women customers are just as important, too. Every piece of meat I sell in here is 'the best one in the house, just special for you, Mrs. Jones.' Every roast that goes over the counter was 'set back just for you, Mrs. Smith.'

"Even when I slice ham for a customer, I make sure that they watch my scales. When I get the exact weight she asked for, I call her attention to it and I say, 'There you are, Mrs. Brown. One pound—16 ounces. But I'll tell you what. Today I'm going to give you a couple of extra slices because you're such an extra special customer of mine.'

"Sure, I charge a nickel a pound more than my competitors do. My meat is better. But my customers are happier than theirs are because mine are getting more than they paid for. They're getting 20 ounces to every pound."

How to Picture Yourself as a Successful Rich Person

Remember that your subconscious mind cannot tell the difference between a real experience and one that you imagine. For this reason, it will store the emotional fantasies you program into it as a reality. For instance, if you see yourself as a great businessman with contracts totaling thousands or millions of dollars annually, you are programming your subconscious mind for success. And its mighty power will answer you with thoughts and ideas of how to make that fantasy come true.

You can visualize yourself driving that new car you want. Or you can imagine seeing yourself owning your own new house. You can fantasize sitting in the living room or the family room surrounded by beautiful furniture, walking on a thick carpet, warming yourself by a huge fireplace. You have the deed to your home locked up in the safety deposit box in the bank. What a comfortable feeling.

You make this programming of your subconscious mind even more realistic when you follow through on your imagined activities: drive the kind of car you've been wanting, talk to a real estate broker about buying the kind of a house that you want. Invest energy and action into the picture that you're programming into your subconscious mind. The more you reinforce that picture with action, the more real it will become. Soon, you won't have to imagine yourself being a success anymore. You'll actually become one when you use the mighty powers of your subconscious mind.

This chapter has been a bit longer than usual. But since becoming successful and rich is the name of the game for almost all of us, I think the extra pages I have used are well-justified.

And now on to the next highly informative and interesting chapter, How You Can Use the Power of Your Subconscious Mind to Rid Yourself of Fears, Worries, and Anxieties Forever.

How You Can Use
the Power of Your
Subconscious Mind to Rid
Yourself of Fears, Worries,
and Anxieties Forever

9

FEAR AND ANXIETY

Most people's fears are imaginary. They never happen to them. Let me give you a classic example of this:

According to an old Arabian fable, Pestilence met a caravan on the road to Baghdad.

"Why are you making such haste to Baghdad?" asked the leader of the caravan.

"To take five thousands lives," Pestilence replied.

On the way back from the city, Pestilence and the caravan met again.

"You lied," the leader said angrily. "You took not five thousand lives, but fifty thousand!"

"No," said Pestilence. "I did not lie. I took only five thousand lives and not one more. *Fear* took all the rest."

Most people are cursed with a variety of fears. For example, one book I saw recently listed 19 fears, including such fears as the worst always happening, thunder and lightning, being in crowds, being alone, meeting people, locked rooms, and on and on.

Most of these fears arise from negative programming of a person's subconscious mind. To get rid of them, a person must reprogram his subconscious mind with positive ideas of courage. One way of doing that would be to do as General George Patton of World War II fame did. When asked if he ever experienced fear before a battle, he replied, "Of course, but I never take counsel of my fears."

Some fears of physical injury can be perfectly valid and are just plain good common sense. If you are at a circus or a zoo and the lions break out of their cages and are running loose through the crowd, you would have a perfect right to feel afraid. Frankly, I would be terrified. Your body's response to legitimate physical fear is the *fight or flight syndrome*, a physiological phenomenon that I will discuss in complete detail in Chapter 11.

Fear Is a Natural Reaction to Any Unknown Situation

First of all, you must realize that fear is your normal and natural reaction to a new, strange, and unknown situation. To solve that problem, you need to gather some facts so you can resolve your fear. Let's look at a specific example of how to do that.

Just suppose that you want to buy a new car, for instance. But you are afraid to do so because you lack the proper information about this situation. You don't know how much your old car is really worth. Nor do you know what that new car should actually cost. What can you do to solve that problem so you can get rid of your fear of doing business with that car salesman? Well, here's what I always do:

I go to the loan department of my bank for accurate and up-to-date information. There I find the current *Blue Book* prices on my own car. Please note that I said *prices* for there are several you should be concerned with.

First of all, you must decide whether your car is in excellent, average, or poor condition. Then you should get the *wholesale cost* (that's how much the dealer would pay at an automobile auction for my old car in its condition), the *retail cost* (that's the price he'd sell it for to someone else after he bought it at the wholesale auction or from me), and the *average loan value*.

The average loan value will always be less than the wholesale cost and my banker, Ed Barlow, tells me that this figure will no doubt be the *starting offer* the dealer will make me for my car.

Ed also tells me that I should deduct from 10 to 15 percent from the *window cost* of the car I want so I can arrive at the dealer's new car cost. This 15 percent can go as high as 19 or 20 percent on an expensive big car like a Lincoln or a Cadillac. And he also says that the dealer's average markup on all those fancy accessories will be at least 20 to 50 percent, sometimes even more than that.

I have in front of me right now a printout from a current car magazine for a new four-door sedan manufactured by one of the divisions of General Motors. The dealer's cost is listed as $10,177. That includes destination charges. The retail cost is $11,754. That is a markup of 15-½ percent, or a profit to the dealer of $1,577. That leaves a lot of room for negotiation. If I can't get that dealer's profit down to between 200 to 400 dollars over his cost, I'll go somewhere else to buy my car.

Now the car dealer is a businessman. So is my banker. Why should my banker be so helpful to me? Shouldn't he be more helpful to another businessman, a comrade-in-arms, you might say. The answer is a resounding no, for my banker wants to loan me the money to buy that new car. Otherwise, he wouldn't be able to make any money for himself.

As you can see from this example, I've been able to get rid of my fear of a new, strange, and unknown situation by gaining knowledge about it that I can use for myself. I am no longer unequipped to do battle with that new car dealer and his salesman. I am no longer handicapped by the fear of ignorance.

You can do the same yourself when you buy a new car. If you don't care to go to a bank or a loan company to get your information, there are numerous magazines published today that will give you accurate information about wholesale and retail costs of new cars. There is absolutely no need for you to go into that car-buying-situation blind and helpless.

This same principle applies to any new, strange, and unknown situation other than buying a car. I used the car example purposely, for being afraid of getting taken in by a car salesman is one of the greatest fears the average person has.

Most Fears Are Psychological, Not Physical

As you can see from this example of buying a new car, most of our fears are psychological rather than physical.

Another psychological fear most people have is the fear of death or injury to someone in the family—a wife or husband, a son or daughter. But death is inevitable. There is no other way out of life. To sit around in fear of when it is going to happen to you or one of your loved ones is but to engage in useless self-torture.

Our nephew, the son of my wife's sister, was killed in a hunting accident a few years ago. His mother and father were grief-stricken, as we all were. But that did not mean that John's parents had lived in fear all those years of this happening. They had enjoyed a happy life together. And that is as it should be with all of us. Life is meant to be enjoyed, not feared.

I could also become overly fearful if I allowed myself to do so, for I have five small granddaughters. If I let myself think about what might happen to them with all of the weirdos running around in today's society, I could become consumed by uncontrollable fear. But rather than let that happen, I program my subconscious mind with positive thoughts that my two sons will do everything in their power to safeguard and protect their daughters. And that is all that I can do.

The Fear of Failure Is Another Common Fear for Most People

The fear of failure usually stems from the fear of criticism. A person fears failure because he fears ridicule and the possibility of being laughed at or made fun of. That's why an unpublished writer will finish his manuscript, lock it up tight in the desk drawer, never to mail it off to a publisher.

When he does this, he's not running the risk of failure and the humiliation of a rejection slip. As long as that manuscript is safe in his desk drawer, he can daydream all day long, pretending to be Hemingway or Faulkner, Steinbeck or whomever his heart desires.

That's also the reason unsuccessful salespeople spend so much time at their desks doing unnecessary paperwork, going on coffee breaks, or just shooting the breeze with each other. They are afraid to get out and make a call on a prospect because they're so terribly afraid of failure.

But to do something is far better than to do nothing, even if sometimes it's wrong. After all, the law of averages will balance things out for you eventually if you will just try. All you need do to be successful is to *act as if it were impossible to fail.* If you do stumble once in a while, that does not mean that you're awkward or clumsy.

For instance, if I get a manuscript back with a rejection slip once in awhile, that doesn't mean that I'm a writing failure. It simply means that one particular manuscript didn't sell at that one specific moment of time. That is the only interpretation I allow myself to put on it.

That, and nothing more than that, for I always act as if it were impossible to fail, too. As long as I feel that way, as long as I program my subconscious mind with such positive thoughts, I will eventually sell everything I write, whether I do it now, next month, or next year.

Since the fear of failure in most people arises from the fear of criticism or ridicule, that is to say, the fear of what others might say or think about them, and since that is the biggest and most common fear for the majority of us, I want to use the rest of this chapter to show you how you can get rid of that fear. When you learn how to do that,

YOU'LL GAIN THESE WORTHWHILE BENEFITS

The biggest benefit you'll gain is freedom from your fear of people and what they might say or think about you. You'll be able to face people with confidence and courage, knowing you don't have to be afraid of anyone or worry about ridicule or criticism from them.

When you put into practice the techniques I'll give you about how to speak up and voice your opinions in front of others, you'll have complete confidence in yourself and your own abilities. No matter who you are or what you do, whether you're a salesperson, a schoolteacher, a store clerk, or a housewife and homemaker, you'll no longer need be afraid of people or what they might think or say about you.

Ralph Waldo Emerson, the American poet, essayist, and philosopher, who lived in the 1800's, once said, "Fear defeats more people than any other thing in the world."

That is ever so true, especially in your daily relationships with others. But it doesn't have to be that way. You don't have to hang onto your fears of people any longer if you don't want to. You can be completely free of your fears, your anxieties, and your worries, and that's a wonderful feeling. As a matter of fact, you will benefit by getting rid of every single one of your fears when you use these . . .

FOUR TECHNIQUES TO GET RID OF YOUR FEARS OF PEOPLE

1. *Admit Your Fear.*

People tend to rationalize to some extent so it's often hard to admit the whole truth, even to themselves. But an unacknowledged fear is the one that can often cause the most trouble for you. You know it's there even when you refuse to admit it. Stuffing your ears with cotton won't make the knock in your car motor go away, no matter how hard you try to pretend it's not there. It's the same with your unadmitted fears.

When you admit your fear, you've taken the first step toward solving your problem. Usually this is the most difficult step for you to take, for most people do not like to admit their fear for they think it is a confession of weakness. But actually the exact opposite is true, for it is an act of courage.

Take an alcoholic, for instance. When he admits that he's powerless over alcohol, as he does in the first step of the Alcoholics Anonymous program, he's on his way to recovery. The same thing happens when you admit your fear to yourself, too. You get it out into the open where you can pin it down and do something about it. Let me give you an example of that:

Frank Gibson, a highly successful paper products salesman, told me how he completely lost his nerve on his first big call on an important leader in the tire and rubber industry, a Mr. Paul Noland.

"As his secretary led me into his luxuriously furnished office, I became increasingly nervous and hesitant," Frank said. "My voice shook as I began to speak. Suddenly I lost my nerve completely and I just couldn't continue. I stood there, perspiring heavily and shaking with fear. Mr. Noland looked up at me in astonishment. Then, without even realizing it, I did the smartest thing I could do. It was a simple little thing that turned my interview from an abject failure into a complete success.

"I mumbled, 'Mr. Noland . . . I . . . uh . . . I've been trying to get in to see you for a long time . . . and . . . uh . . . now that I'm finally here, I'm so nervous and afraid I can't even talk!'

"But when I spoke, to my surprise, my fear began to leave me. My head quickly cleared, my hands and my knees stopped shaking. Mr. Noland suddenly seemed to become my friend. He seemed extremely pleased that I should look at him as such an important person."

As Frank went on to say, this was an important turning point in his career as a salesman. He found that by admitting his fear he was able to take the first step in conquering it. You can do the same if you will just remember this one simple rule which constitutes the first of the four steps you can use to get rid of your fear: *When you're afraid, admit it.*

Just admit to yourself, once and for all, that you do have this specific fear and more than half your problem will be solved. Once you've done that, you can move on to the next step:

2. *Analyze Your Fear to See If It's Really Justified.*

After you've admitted to yourself exactly what it is that you are afraid of, then you need to analyze your fear to see if it is truly justified. If it is, then you can do something about solving it. If it is not justified, you can stop worrying about it immediately.

Let's first look at unjustified or imaginary fear. Here is an example of what it can do to a person.

"I used to be afraid to speak up in a staff conference," Christina Davis says. "I thought my ideas might sound stupid and people would laugh at me. I was afraid my thoughts were not well enough organized to present at a meeting. And then I always felt that someone else might have a better idea.

"But when I heard others offer the same idea I'd had and no one laughed, I realized that my fears were not justified. They were entirely imaginary and self-generated. Now I speak up and say what I think without hesitation and no one laughs at me or at my ideas and suggestions."

Now then. Let's talk about you. Is your fear because of something bad that has happened to you in the past? Have you had some unfortunate previous experience? We've all had them. They are over and done with; forget them.

Or perhaps your fear is based on a false assumption just as Christina's was. For example, maybe you're afraid of your boss as so many people are. Why should you be? Are you afraid he's going to raise Cain with you for something you've done wrong? Why? Have you made some terrible mistake that will cause your boss to lose money? Are you afraid he's going to fire you? Why? Do you deserve to be fired? Has your work been sloppy and inefficient? Do you come into work late all the time? Have you been stealing from your boss? If your answer to all these questions is "No," then you have nothing at all to worry about. You're giving yourself stomach ulcers and cardiac flutter for no good reason at all.

What do you do if your fear is justified? For instance, are you afraid you won't get promoted because you lack knowledge? Then do the obvious thing you need to do. Gain the proper knowledge.

Or if you are afraid your people might let you down, you can do as Steve Olson, a district sales manager, did.

"I was always afraid some of my branch salespeople would make some bad mistakes in handling some of our big accounts," Steve said. "Part of my fear was justified because serious mistakes were possible. So I decided to do everything I could to prevent errors and then to stop worrying about it altogether.

"First, I made sure all my salespeople were well-trained. Next, I made up a corrective plan of action just in case something did go wrong. Third, I realized that further worrying on my part about the potential problem was futile. It was a complete waste of my time and energy. Today, I take things just as they come, one thing at a time, one day at a time. Everything seems to be completely manageable to me now."

Steve is so right in his approach. If your fear is justified, then do whatever you can to eliminate your fear. Then stop worrying about it. You cannot control the whole world. A tornado, an earthquake, even a drunken driver can cause a tragedy in your life. You must simply learn not to worry about those things in life which you cannot change. Don't program your subconscious mind with such negative thoughts.

3. *Take the Necessary Action to Get Rid of Your Fear.*

The third step in conquering your fear is to translate your analysis into the necessary action. And some kind of action is required, for no action at all is usually more detrimental than too much activity.

If you are afraid and take no action whatever to control or conquer your fear, you will never be able to overcome it. For instance, the person who is afraid of everything—learning to swim, driving a car, getting married, buying a home, starting his own business—never will be able to overcome his fears of doing anything unless he does something positive about them. To conquer your fear, you must take definite, concrete action of some kind.

I told you previously that one of the best ways to succeed was to act as if it were impossible to fail. That technique is valuable in overcoming your fears so you can use it here. But in addition to that technique, there are two additional methods that you can use. These are (a) Don't concentrate on what you fear, (b) Do the thing you fear to do and you'll have the power to do it.

a. *Don't concentrate on what you fear.*

Fear requires you to have an active imagination. Don't exaggerate fear in your mind. Your imagination can turn fishworms into snakes and lizards into dragons.

Remember that Job said, "For the thing which I greatly feared is come upon me, and that which I was afraid of is come unto me" (Job 3:25). So take a lesson from his experience. Keep in mind that whenever you fear anything, that thing is much more likely to find you and harm you.

"As a man thinketh in his heart so is he," wrote James Allen, the

19th century English author, and today his tiny book, *As a Man Thinketh*, containing those words is a classic.

Time and again it's been proven over and over. *You really do become or you really do get what you think about.* Think about love and you will be loved for you will project love to others. Think about hate and that is exactly what you will get, hate, for that is what you will project to others. Concentrate on poverty and you will be poor for you will attract poverty to you. Nothing can prevent it. If you fear failure and constantly think about it, you will fail. Absolutely nothing can keep it from happening. Worry about criticism and ridicule from others and you will be criticized and ridiculed, for your excessive worry will cause you to make stupid and ridiculous mistakes.

To keep these things from happening to you, program your subconscious mind with positive thoughts instead of negative ones. *Don't think about what you fear.* Instead, concentrate on the solution to the problem rather than on the problem itself. If you fear failure—concentrate on how to be successful. If you are afraid of being poor—think only of wealth and abundance.

Or when it comes to listening to criticism from others, please keep this thought in mind. It is one thing to listen to the words of a qualified person *when you've asked for his advice.* But it is quite another when you allow unsolicited adverse criticism from people to program your subconscious mind with negative ideas that can cause you to fail. Get rid of your fear of that kind of criticism right now and drive straight ahead toward your goal.

b. Do the thing you fear to do and you'll gain the power to do it.

The second method you can use when you take the necessary action to get rid of your fear is to *do the thing you fear to do so you will gain the power to do it.* Now doing the thing you fear to do so you will have the power to do it is not really man's idea alone. It is also a law of nature. For instance, I have watched birds fly and I always figured it was automatic for them to do so. But that is not true at all. Let me tell you why I know that.

Last year a robin built a nest in the tree just outside my study window. I watched the growth of this robin's family, from the eggs in the nest until the day that four little heads popped up demanding to be fed. And then one by one, the mother robin nudged her babies off into the air to fly when the right time came.

But one little fellow was so afraid that he couldn't fly. It took him nearly a week longer than the others. Finally the mother had to force him out of the nest. And when she did, he suddenly flapped his wings and flew awkwardly away. No one had taught him to fly at all. Nature had put the instinct there for him to do it. But he had to fly first before he had the power to do it, for that is nature's law; her way of doing things. The same is true for you. You must do the thing you fear to do so you will have the power to do it. But if you will not do the thing you fear to do, you will never gain the power to do it. Honestly now, it's just that simple.

For instance, if you want to be a painter—then you must paint. There simply is no other way to become an artist. You can dream all day long about how famous and how successful you are as a painter, but until you pick up the brush and start painting, you will never gain the power to do it.

If you want to be a writer—then you must write. If you want to be an expert swimmer—then you must swim. The same can be said for golf, baseball, salesmanship, science, medicine, law, music, and so on. You must make the first move yourself. Until you do that, you will never gain the power to do anything.

So if there do happen to be certain things in your life that you actually fear to do, then force yourself to do them until you've reached the point you are no longer afraid. And that, by the way, is the real definition of courage: the control of fear. Courage is not the absence of fear as so many people believe. It is the control of fear.

4. *How to Overcome Your Fears of Speaking Up or Voicing Your Opinion in Public.*

I know that speaking in public strikes fear into the hearts of nearly everyone at first. I know I nearly panicked the first time I stood up in front of a large audience. My throat was dry; my voice was raspy. My palms were sweaty—my heart was pounding.

But when I spoke the first sentence, I immediately began to feel better. As I continued to speak, my fears faded away. Confidence came back to me, for as soon as I did the thing I feared so much to do, I gained the power to do it.

I have for many years now given seminars and lectures to people showing them how to get up the courage to speak their piece and voice their opinions in public. Before I give you the specific techniques you can use to do that, too, I want to quote for you from a few letters I've received from people who've attended my seminars.

Gary J., an Orlando, Florida, salesman, wrote me to say, "After I heard your talk on how to get rid of your fear of people, I felt I could take on anyone. Yesterday I walked into the office of a really tough purchasing agent—a man I'd always feared and who'd never once given me an order. Before he could say 'No,' I had my samples spread out on his desk. First time I'd ever opened my sample case in his office. He gave me one of the biggest orders I've ever received. Why? Because my attitude was positive and confident. I was no longer afraid of him and he knew it."

Gail R., a bashful Jacksonville, Florida salesclerk, wrote me this: "I was so afraid of customers I gave them the feeling I was apologizing to them for waiting on them. I was even afraid to come to hear your lecture. I thought someone I knew might see me there and laugh at me. Then I was scared to death to try your idea of doing the thing I feared to do so I would have the power to do it, but I really had no other choice in the matter. The sales manager had given me exactly three weeks to get my sales up to par with the other clerks or lose my job.

"But the moment I did as you said, I found I was suddenly speaking to customers with more assurance. My poise and self-confidence increased. I began to answer objections and questions with authority. My sales went up nearly 40 percent last month. There's never been another word said about my dismissal. In fact, the store manager told me to start thinking about taking over the management of one of the departments."

Nancy L., a Miami housewife, wrote me to say, "I was afraid to invite my friends in for coffee for fear I wouldn't be able to keep a conversation going. But after listening to your talk at our church last Wednesday night, I took the plunge and held a coffee call for half a dozen of my neighbors today. It was a huge success. I had no trouble at all keeping things moving along interesting lines of conversation. Thanks so much for your help."

Now I want to give you eight pointers that will help you even further in getting rid of your fears of speaking up or voicing your opinion in front of a large audience. When you use them, you'll be able to stand up in front of any group of people, say what you want to say without fear and trepidation, be that group your Sunday school class, a PTA meeting, a meeting of the town council, a union meeting, whatever.

By developing confidence in your ability to speak up in front of people, you'll lose your fear of doing that and that's what we're really after here. As a friend of mine, Bill R., put it, "I used to be afraid to say anything at all about what I thought about a subject. No more after what you told me, Jim. I may not be an authority on the subject under discussion, but I'll give an opinion on it, you can bet on that."

When you use the eight pointers I'm going to give you, you'll be programming your subconscious mind for success. Here, then, are the eight pointers that will help you as much as they helped Bill R.

1. *You Are Not Alone.*

The person who isn't a bit nervous about speaking in public is as rare as a blacksmith or a good cribbage player. A midwestern university conducted a survey of its speech classes and found that most of their students suffered from some stage fright at both the beginning and at the end of the course. However, the speech classes had helped the students to control that stage fright and not let it take over completely.

2. *A Certain Amount of Nervousness is Useful.*

It is quite normal for a person to be slightly nervous just before he speaks to an audience. This is how the body prepares itself for this strange, new, and unknown situation. Your pulse beats faster, your breathing speeds up, your muscles tense. Don't be alarmed at all about this; it's just nature's way of doing things.

By understanding the basic physiological functions of your own body, you can keep this normal preparatory nervous tension from developing into uncontrollable panic, just as those students did. That extra shot of adrenalin will help you to think faster, to talk more easily, and to speak with greater emphasis and intensity than under ordinary normal circumstances.

3. *Even Experienced Professionals Are Nervous at First.*

Could be that you've heard famous TV and movie personalities admit that they always have a certain amount of stage fright just before they go on and that it lasts for the first few minutes of the performance. And professional speakers who earn their living speaking to large audiences will tell you the same thing.

"A certain amount of nervous tension is always present before I start to speak," says Martin Erskine. "It lasts through the first few sentences of my talk. This is part of the price I pay for being in my profession; it's an occupational hazard. But if I were not built that way, I doubt seriously if I'd ever be a good speaker."

Martin is an old-timer in this business. He has traveled more than a million miles and spoken to thousands and thousands of people during his highly successful career and he is still going strong.

Martin is also a member of a speech faculty at a midwestern university, holds a BA in speech from a California university, a Master's degree in speech from Ohio State, yet he says he still gets a bit nervous when he first walks out on the platform. The important thing is that he knows how to control it and his nervousness doesn't last very long.

4. *One Reason You Are Afraid Is Lack of Experience.*

There is a great deal of difference between this normal nervous tension almost all good speakers have and a deep, uncontrollable fear of speaking in public.

But practice makes perfect in speaking up before others just the same as in learning to drive a car, dance, play the guitar, or ride a bicycle. So at the risk of being monotonous and repetitious, I must say to you once more: do the thing you fear to do and you'll gain the power to do it. And the more you do it, the better you'll become and the greater will be your confidence in yourself to speak up.

5. *Don't Memorize Your Talk Word for Word.*

There is nothing wrong with memorizing certain key phrases, but to memorize everything you want to say is but to invite total disaster. If you for only one split second forget where you are in your prepared remarks, you're dead.

The best way to memorize, if you must, is to memorize only certain key points. However, let me say that if your talk has a natural continuity, even that will become unnecessary, since you can easily move from one idea to the next. All you need do is arrange your ideas in a logical sequence before you get up to speak.

6. *Rehearse Your Talk First.*

This one point often marks the major difference between the professional public speaker and the amateur. It can also separate the successful talk from the unsuccessful one, too.

The most successful public speakers always rehearse their talks first in front of a mirror. Remember I told you that even Winston Churchill did that and he was one of the most compelling speakers ever known. If you have a tape recorder, dictate your comments or your talk into it. I always do that. A lot of mistakes I didn't hear when I spoke come back to me magnified when I listen to myself.

7. *Know Your Subject and Stick To It.*

This is another point that often separates the professional from the amateur. The amateur often tries to know everything about everything. Don't do it, for it can't be done. Learn only the subject you want to discuss or speak about and stick to that. Then you can appear to be an expert. Remember that you are an expert only as long as you stick to your own line.

8. *Concentrate Only on the Job to Be Done.*

Forget yourself and concentrate only on your subject. If you start worrying about errors in grammar or the possibility you might come to the end of your time before you've covered all the points you want to, you can destroy your self-confidence even before you start. Just concentrate on your message, say what you want to get across to your audience, and you'll make it through to the end in fine shape.

Why Preparation for the Worst Is Not Fear

This is the last point I want to cover in this chapter. Preparation for the worst is not fear, it is only common sense. As Dionysius, the ancient Greek, once said, "Forethought is better than repentance."

Many years ago I made several trips across Arizona and New Mexico. In those days, filling stations and rest stops were not as plentiful as they are now, so we always carried two water bags on the front of the car for emergencies. Fear never entered my mind when we did this; it was only proper preparation.

Today, I live in Florida, hurricane country, so we prepare for the worst here, too. All our windows have hurricane shutters that can be closed tight. When a warning comes of an approaching storm, we stock up on a supply of canned goods, candles, and fresh water.

Insurance, whether it's life, car, or house, is also preparation for the worst. Again, it is not fear, but only common sense to prepare for disaster.

Rather than stew and fret and worry about what might happen, prepare for the worst, and then forget it. Sit back and relax knowing that you've done all that can be done. This whole idea might be best summed up this way: Expect the best, but prepare for the worst.

And now on to Chapter 10, where I'll show you how you can rid yourself of any undesirable habits you might have by properly programming your subconscious mind.

How You Can Use the Mighty Power of Your Subconscious Mind to Rid Yourself of Undesirable Habits

10

If I were to ask you which was more important in breaking a bad habit, *imagination* or *willpower*, you would probably say willpower. Almost everyone does. But that is not the correct answer. Using your imagination is the only way you can break a bad habit, and here's why:

Just suppose, for example, you make a New Year's resolution to stop smoking as so many people do. You are determined to quit by using your willpower and proving that you are stronger than that little white cigarette.

So you say to yourself, "I am not going to smoke . . . I am not going to smoke . . . I am not going to smoke." You repeat this to yourself over and over again using willpower, while all the time your imagination is telling you how a good cigarette would taste.

As long as you allow your imagination to tell you how good that cigarette would taste, sooner or later, and usually sooner, you will light up a cigarette and smoke again. Why? The answer is quite simple.

Whenever imagination and willpower are in conflict with each other— whenever they are pulling in opposite directions—imagination will always win.

But when the imagination and willpower are in agreement with each other, when they are harmoniously pulling in the same direction, an irresistible force is created, and success is always the inevitable result.

I will use this chapter to show you how to get your willpower and your imagination working together and pulling in the same direction by programming your subconscious mind properly so you can stop smoking, step excessive drinking, quit overeating, stop putting things off until tomorrow, get rid of a bad temper, eliminate laziness, or whatever other bad habit is troubling you.

THE ONE BIG BENEFIT YOU'LL GAIN FROM THIS CHAPTER

There are a variety of benefits I could mention dependent upon whatever bad habit you're getting rid of. However, the one big benefit you'll gain when you break an undesirable habit is *freedom*. You'll no longer be a captive of your habit; you'll no longer be its slave.

FIVE TECHNIQUES TO BE USED ON ALL BAD HABITS

The general techniques I'm going to list now can be used to solve any bad habit you want to get rid of, no matter what it is. I will discuss these five techniques first. Then I'll show you how to apply them so you can resolve any bad habit, be it smoking, overeating, excessive drinking, procrastination, a bad temper, whatever.

1. *You Must Reach the Point You Can No Longer Tolerate Yourself the Way You Are or the Situation the Way It Is.*
Let me give you a specific example of what I mean by this:
A male alcoholic's wife, children, friends, business associates, and boss all reach the point where they can no longer tolerate him the way he is long before he does. But that male alcoholic will never stop drinking despite all the pleas from others until he, himself, reaches the point he can no longer tolerate himself the way he is. When he does reach that point, he will stop drinking, but not before. Let me show you exactly what I mean by that.

A man who'd been drunk every night for many years arrived home late, bombed out of his skull again. The next morning his wife found him staring at himself in the mirror. He turned to her and said, "I'm giving up drinking; I'm through with it. I can't take it any longer. I'm sick and tired of being sick and tired."

Then he placed a bottle of beer on the mantlepiece.

"Why are you doing that?" his wife asked.

"That's just so I know where to find a drink if I want one," he said. "Then I can just kill myself instead!"

He has not touched a drink for more than 10 years now, but the bottle of beer still sits on the mantlepiece as a reminder of his previous intolerable situation.

Although his wife had pleaded with him for many years to stop drinking, he had never paid any attention to her. It was not until he reached the point he could stand himself no longer the way he was that he did something about his bad habit.

2. *You Must Want to Be Free of Your Bad Habit More than You Want to Hang onto It.*

Every person with a bad habit that he wants to break always has mixed emotions about it. He may want to break his bad habit—say smoking, for example—but by the same token he does not want to give it up. He will never quit until he wants to be free of his smoking habit more than he wants to keep it. Sometimes the motivator is better health, sometimes money, sometimes just plain disgust with himself. Here's an example of that:

Roy, noting that the price of cigarettes had gone up again, complained loudly, but he still put the extra dime in the vending machine. A coworker laughed at him. "You'll pay whatever they ask," he said. "You have no choice. They've got you hooked."

"My God, he's right," Roy thought. "The tobacco company has me exactly where it wants me. I'm no longer free. I'm a slave to this stinking habit. To hell with it." So then and there, he quit his three-pack-a-day habit forever.

3. *You Must Establish Tangible and Concrete Goals to Be Reached.*

This can best be done by listing all the benefits that will be yours when you are rid of your bad habit. You can further motivate yourself by listing all the disadvantages that will be yours if you insist on hanging onto your undesirable habit.

4. *You Must Reprogram Your Subconscious Mind with These New Concepts, Attitudes, and Ideas.*

Remember that your conscious mind furnishes the willpower necessary to take only the first step in breaking your bad habit. It makes the decision to do so, but that is as far as it can go. Before you can break your bad habit, you must use your imagination to reprogram your subconscious mind with positive thoughts of benefits that will overcome and override the negative input that caused your bad habit in the first place.

Program all these benefits into your subconscious mind until you become obsessed with the idea of freedom from your undesirable habit. As a recovered alcoholic, Carl S., once told me, "I used to have an obsession to drink . . . now I have an obsession to stay sober." Now that's the kind of desire to break a bad habit that I'm talking about.

5. *Do It One Day at a Time*.

Another helpful concept I learned from Carl is to solve a bad habit exactly one day at a time. As Carl says, "I didn't have to quit drinking forever. I don't think I could've done that, for that's too long a period of time. In fact, forever is impossible for an alcoholic to conceive. So we just quit drinking for one day at a time. And since tomorrow never comes, it's always today. I know that's a gimmick, but it works to keep an alcoholic from drinking, and that's the whole purpose of the Alcoholics Anonymous program, to help the alcoholic who has a desire to stop drinking."

This fifth technique will work for other bad habits as well as excessive drinking, such as smoking, loss of weight, a bad temper, whatever. If an alcoholic can go one day without a drink, then a smoker can go one day without a cigarette, a fat person can go one day without overeating, and so on. Those days can turn into weeks, weeks into months, and before too long, your bad habit has been completely broken.

With these five general techniques firmly in mind, let's now move on to certain specific bad habits that you might want to get rid of. Let's start with one of the easier ones first.

How You Can Get Rid of the Procrastination Habit

If procrastination is one of your major problems, you are not alone. It has been estimated that this habit afflicts 90 to 95 percent of us. Why do people procrastinate? Because we would rather do what we like to do and put off until tomorrow, or preferably next week or even next month—maybe if we're lucky, even forever—those things we don't like to do. Let me give you a specific example of procrastination.

Marjorie is a real estate saleswoman. Some of her time is spent on the telephone to locate potential customers although she dislikes this procedure a great deal. One rainy afternoon she decides to do some telephone prospecting since the weather is too bad to go outside.

She sits down with a street directory which lists streets and house numbers and then the names in reverse of the way the telephone directory is made up. She sits for a while staring at a page opened to one of the streets in her territory and then decides to have a cup of coffee first. That leads to scanning the newspaper with her coffee and a pleasant 20 or 30 minutes is passed before she forces herself back to the directory.

After another 10 minutes of looking at names, she finally dials a number and to her joy, the line is busy. What's going on here anyway? Well, Marjorie decided by force of willpower to do some telemarketing, but her imagination is working against her instead of with her. She keeps imagining that the person who answers the phone is going to be rude and ill-tempered so she hesitates to make that call.

To rid herself of this fear of rejection, all she needs to do is let her imagination and willpower work together believing that the person who answers is going to be pleasant and good-natured. Ninety-five times out of a hundred, this will be the case. Marjorie can dismiss the other five who are grouchy or ill-tempered by feeling sorry for them and being thankful that her disposition isn't like that.

Now if you think you don't have this bad habit of putting things off, just as Marjorie does, let me ask you this:

1. Do you do something you prefer to do instead of doing what you know you should be doing?

2. Do you conveniently put the required work out of sight so you can't be reminded of it?

3. Do you tell yourself that you need to rest and relax?

4. Do you get sick or half-sick, and therefore decide you just aren't well enough to do the job until tomorrow?

5. Do you manage to be late for work and then convince yourself that there's not enough time to do the job today?

6. Do you conveniently forget to bring the proper materials along that are necessary to complete the job; for instance, data sheets, time charts, sales figures, etc.?

If you answered *yes* to any of these questions, you are guilty of putting things off, too. How deeply rooted this procrastination habit is can be determined by the number of *yes* answers that you gave. If you answered all six affirmatively, then you really need to reprogram your subconscious mind in a big way to get out of your procrastination rut.

One of the major reasons people procrastinate and put things off is that they are afraid of making the wrong decision. As the American philosopher, Walter Kaufmann, once said, "Most people suffer from *decidophobia*." There are three major reasons for this kind of procrastination.

1. *The Need to Always Be Right*. Some people can't make up their minds about even such minor matters as which movie to go see, which

television program to watch, or where to go on a vacation, because they are too afraid of making a mistake. So they procrastinate and do nothing. It is not that the decision to be made is a matter of life or death. It is simply that the person cannot bear the idea of being wrong.

2. *Mixing Objective Facts with Subjective Opinions.* Most decisions can be made on the basis of objective facts. Very few can be made only on subjective feelings. When these two are not kept separate, it is hard to make a rational decision, so the person procrastinates and puts things off.

3. *The Fear of Permanent Commitment.* Some people feel that once a decision is made, it is fixed and irrevocable. Not true. If you make a wrong decision, the simple way out is to make another decision to correct it.

Two Examples of Procrastination and Indecisiveness

1. When Mildred was 16, her parents gave her a yearly clothing allowance and told her she could make all her own purchases. Mildred was delighted until she had to make her first buying decision on her own. She became so worried about making the wrong choice and displeasing her parents that she ended up buying nothing and went back to her mother for help.

2. Doris decided to go back to work when her daughter entered junior high. She was offered three good jobs, but she couldn't decide which one to take. After two weeks of agonizing and putting things off, she finally made up her mind, but by then it was too late. All three jobs had been filled and were gone.

Guidelines to Making the Right Decision

You can rid yourself of the procrastination habit in making decisions if you will follow these simple guidelines:

1. *Learn to be positive in all your actions.* Don't delay; don't beat around the bush. Remember that it takes more energy to fail than it does to succeed. Act as if it were impossible to fail and you will always succeed.

2. *Get the facts you need, make up your mind,* and then proceed with complete confidence that you are right.

3. *Give yourself a reasonable deadline* for making your decision. A

specific deadline forces you to come to grips with the facts and helps you break the procrastination habit.

4. *Limit your choices.* If you are picking out a new carpet, for example, and you are confused by the wide number of choices available, narrow them down by looking at only three at a time and picking the best one. Then look at the next three and pick the best one, and so on. Then take the best ones you've already picked and repeat this same process until eventually you will have only one left. You can use this same method to pick out your suits, shoes, dresses, ties, furniture, and so on.

5. *Recheck decisions* you have made to see if they were sound and timely.

6. *Analyze decisions made by others.* If you do not agree with them, determine if your reasons for disagreement are both sound and logical.

7. *Broaden your viewpoint* by studying the actions of others so you can profit from their successes or from their failures.

8. *Don't make major decisions on minor matters.* Save your real efforts for the big and important decisions you have to make. Don't give yourself a migraine headache trying to decide whether to have string beans or asparagus for dinner.

9. *Do the thing you fear to do* and you'll gain the power to do it. When you do the thing you fear to do, you will suddenly discover that your fear was completely unjustified. Therefore, there is no real reason for procrastination.

10. *Program your subconscious mind with success ideas* and your procrastination habit will disappear automatically for you'll have no reason to put things off any longer.

Since procrastination is so often involved in getting rid of the bad habits of smoking, excessive drinking, overeating, or a rotten temper, covering it first will help you in conquering these others, if you have any of them. Now let's take up a habit that is of great concern to many people, that of smoking.

How to Stop Smoking Cold Turkey

First of all, I'd like to review quickly for you the five general techniques to be used on all bad habits so you can put them to work here for yourself. Again, they are:

1. You must reach the point you can no longer tolerate yourself the way you are or the situation the way that it is.

2. You must want to be free of your bad habit more than you want to hang onto it.

3. You must establish tangible and concrete goals to be reached or benefits to be achieved.

4. You must reprogram your subconscious mind with new and positive concepts, attitudes, and ideas.

5. Do it only one day at a time.

Fear can be one of the biggest motivators in giving up cigarettes. Remember that fear is always on the opposite side of the coin of desire. You want to smoke, but the fear of cancer, heart attack, bronchitis, asthma, and emphysema must be stronger than your desire for a cigarette. This is one time when fear can be beneficial to you.

For example, I smoked three to four packs of cigarettes every day until I was 45 years old, even though I was a doctor and I knew better. One morning I woke up with a tremendous pain in my chest. I felt as if someone had thrown a huge spear through my chest and it had gone all the way through and was coming out of my back.

This horrible pain persisted for five days, yet I continued to smoke in spite of it. On the sixth day, I made the decision to stop smoking and I did just that for I had finally reached the point that I wanted to quit more than I wanted to smoke. I was scared to death of possible lung cancer. That has been more than 20 years ago and I have not touched a single cigarette since then.

The pain in my chest disappeared within 10 days and has never come back. My lungs are clean and clear. X-rays show them to be as healthy as the lungs of a person who has never smoked. I have more energy and my food tastes better. All in all, the benefits of not smoking far outweigh the benefits—if indeed there are any at all—of smoking.

My daughter-in-law also gave up cigarettes because of fear. Her doctor had warned her that she had an irregular heart beat because of cigarettes, and she, too, quit smoking cold turkey because of fear several years ago. She has never smoked again.

Sometimes vanity is the answer. Our daughter, Teresa, had also smoked for a number of years. One day she read a magazine article that said that women who smoked have more wrinkles at 50 than nonsmokers do at 70.

Immediately after reading this article she went to the supermarket and there she saw a little old woman sitting on a bench waiting for the bus and smoking. As Teresa said later, "That woman had more wrinkles than I've ever seen. She had wrinkles on top of wrinkles."

She has never smoked another cigarette and that has been more than 10 years ago. As she said, "If smoking makes you look like that, it just isn't worth it."

I had sent her articles on the dangers and hazards of smoking and potential lung cancer for years with no effect. But one glimpse of what she might look like if she kept on smoking was enough to make her stop. In her case, vanity was a bigger motivator than fear.

Whatever your motivation, you must list all the benefits you can think of to convince yourself that it is more worthwhile to quit than it is to continue smoking. I know I mentioned back in Chapter 7 some of the many benefits you could gain for yourself when you stop smoking, but giving up the cigarette habit is so important to your health, they are well worth repeating here. For example, when you quit,

1. You'll no longer have that hacking smoker's cough that is so annoying to yourself and to everyone else as well.

2. You'll not run the risk of excessive facial wrinkles, an important benefit to consider, not only for a woman, but also for a man.

3. Your lungs will heal rapidly and you'll no longer run the increased risk of cancer, bronchitis, asthma, and emphysema.

4. You'll greatly reduce the risk of heart attack.

5. You'll cut down the strain on your vascular system and lower your blood pressure which reduces the risk of a crippling stroke.

6. Your food will smell better as well as taste better, for smoking impairs not only your sense of taste, but also, your sense of smell.

7. You'll save money. A two-pack-a-day-habit at one dollar a pack will cost you more than $700 a year. I don't know about you, but that represents a healthy sum of money to me.

8. You'll live longer. Insurance statistics show that a nonsmoker's lifespan is much longer than that of a smoker. Not only will you live longer, but your life will be much more enjoyable as well.

9. You'll be free! This is one of the biggest benefits—to be free to choose. When you are addicted with the cigarette habit, you have no choice in the matter. You have to smoke. When you're free of the habit, you're also free to make the decision to smoke or not to smoke, and that's a wonderful feeling of relief.

Now that is a tremendous number of benefits to gain when you give up smoking. So instead of trying to quit by using the willpower of your conscious mind, use your imagination and program your subconscious mind with all these benefits and you will succeed this time even if you've failed many times before. When imagination and willpower work together and are pulling in the same direction aimed toward the same goal, an irresistible force is created. Success is then inevitable.

How to Stop Overeating if That's Your Problem

Talk show host Merv Griffin watched a comedian imitating him—as a fat man. The comic had stuffed himself with padding and Griffin could not stand the caricature of himself. So he went on a diet and exercise program, and soon was able to show off his new slim body to his audience. Why the change? Merv had reached his bottom . . . the point where he could no longer tolerate himself the way he was. That's when he decided to do something about it.

During the 30 and more years I practiced chiropractic, I helped hundreds of people to lose weight with my *non-glue-food* diet.* For some, the motivating factor in losing excess weight was better health; for others, just as in smoking, it was vanity.

But no matter what the motivation, just as in breaking the smoking habit, willpower is *not* the key to success. You must use your imagination to dream up all the possible benefits you can gain and program them into your subconscious mind so you can lose those unwanted pounds. Let me list some of these benefits for you here:

1. You'll have more energy, more vitality, more pep and go-power. You'll no longer be short of breath.

2. Your complexion will be clear; your hair will shine.

3. You'll be regular without laxatives; your digestion will improve; you'll be free from heartburn and acid stomach.

4. You'll not be nervous and highstrung; you'll even sleep better.

5. If you are a woman, people will mistake you for your daughter.

6. Also, if you are a woman, you won't have to make any excuses for your figure, even when you wear a scanty swimsuit at the beach or pool.

7. You can be the envy of all your "plump" friends.

8. You'll look and feel five to ten years younger.

---

*James K. Van Fleet, *Doctor Van Fleet's Amazing New Non-Glue-Food Diet* (West Nyack, New York, Parker Publishing Company, 1974).

9. Your sex life will improve dramatically.
10. You'll run far less risk of a heart attack.
11. Your blood pressure will be much lower.
12. Your circulation will improve markedly.
13. According to insurance statistics, you'll live much longer.
14. Your low, nagging backache will disappear.
15. Your arthritis and rheumatism will be much less painful.
16. Life will definitely become worthwhile living once again.

Now that's a carload of benefits you can gain when you get rid of your excess weight. And you don't have to use willpower to do it. In fact, you can't, as I'll show you in just a moment. You must use your imagination and program your subconscious mind with all these benefits that can be yours when you slim down. Then losing weight will become easy for you.

As further motivation, you can program your subconscious mind with pictures just as one of my overweight patients, Lucille, did. She scotchtaped two pictures of herself to her refrigerator door. One showed what she looked like when she graduated from high school and was a slim 115 pounds. The other was a current one with her weight at 190 pounds. It took her six months to get rid of 75 pounds, but she succeeded for she was motivated by what she saw staring at her from her refrigerator door.

Why Willpower Will not Work for You

You cannot use willpower to get rid of your excess weight any more than one of my patients, Irene, could. Let me tell you about her experience. Irene continued to fight her problem by trying to use willpower to conquer it.

You see, she wanted to prove to herself that she had the willpower to resist her desire for sweets, so she put a box of chocolates on the dining room table and then sat down to stare glumly at them, vowing all the time to herself not to touch a single one.

The outcome of this? She ate the entire box of candy, of course. What else could she do? Under such circumstances, she really had no other choice.

But today she's thin. She's no longer carrying around her excess fat. She got rid of it after she learned not to use willpower, but to use her imagination properly to concentrate on the benefits she would gain by losing her extra pounds.

When you fight your problem of excess fat—or any other problem you have—the way Irene did, when you antagonize any unfavorable situation and allow it to tempt you, you are programming your subconscious mind with the wrong goals. In doing that, you simply give your problem more power over you. You deplete your own power to gain victory to that same extent. Many times, especially at first glance, resistance seems to be the only way out of your dilemma.

However, you will find that bombarding your problem with willpower could easily cause you to be stuck with it. The opposite course—nonresistance—is the only way out. An alcoholic, for example, uses nonresistance to stop drinking when he finally admits he's powerless over alcohol and gives up the battle of trying to control his drinking. That is the real meaning of the phrase, "Resist not evil," from the Sermon on the Mount. (Matthew 5:39)

When you do not fight your problem with willpower, but instead use your imagination to visualize all the benefits you'll receive when you attain your goal, your problem will crumble away and disappear for you.

You might ask, then, what use is willpower? It is useful in only one way: making the initial decision to change, whether that change is to lose weight, stop smoking, quit drinking, putting things off, getting rid of a bad temper, whatever. Once that decision is made with willpower, then you must use your imagination to program your subconscious mind with the benefits you'll receive so you can make that decision you made with willpower stick.

Remember, as I told you earlier, when imagination and willpower are in agreement with each other, when they are harmoniously pulling in the same direction, an irresistible force is created, and success is always the inevitable result.

How to Stop Excessive Drinking

You may not realize it, but no less than one out of every 13 people who drink is troubled with the problem of excessive drinking, in many cases, the actual disease of alcoholism.

Now, as I mentioned before, the male alcoholic's wife, children, friends, business associates, and boss all reach the point they can no longer tolerate him the way he is long before he does.

That male alcoholic will never stop drinking until he, himself, reaches the point he can no longer tolerate himself the way he is. When he does finally reach that point, he will stop drinking, but not before.

My friend, Carl, that recovered alcoholic who is a member of Alcoholics Anonymous, puts it this way: "An alcoholic will drink until he hits his bottom, wherever that is," Carl says. "Some alcoholics have a higher bottom than others, as we say. One guy might still have his wife, his children, his home, even his job when he finally hits his bottom. But another might have lost everything and be completely down and out on skid row before he reaches the point he can no longer stand himself the way he is. But in both cases, the person has to hit his own bottom, whatever that is, before he will ever make any attempt to change."

I asked Carl how the A. A. program motivates a newcomer to get sober. Here's what he told me:

"We tell the new person all about the benefits he'll gain when he stops drinking. There are a whole slug of them. Just for instance, he'll never have to suffer from another hangover. There won't be any rubber checks to worry about. He'll always remember where he parked his car. He won't have to throw up in the toilet every morning. Nor will he fall down anymore and rip the knees out of a new pair of pants as I always used to do.

"Some other big benefits he'll realize are never running the risk of driving his car while he's drunk and killing someone else in an automobile accident. He won't need to panic every time he hears a siren or sees the red light on the police cruiser that's going around him. He'll never run the risk of hallucinations or delirium tremens. Nor will he be in danger anymore of cirrhosis of the liver or becoming a wet-brain or a living vegetable as so many alcoholics do. And he won't have to worry about killing himself, either accidentally when he's drunk or purposely when he's sober.

"There are a lot more benefits like regaining the love and respect of your wife and children, your friends, and your boss as well as dignity and respect for yourself, but I think I've given you enough for starters."

If drinking too much is a problem for you and it is causing you definite trouble, look over that long list of benefits Carl mentioned so you can convince yourself of the advantages of sobriety. Then program your subconscious mind with those positive benefits so you can convince yourself that you are better off not to drink than to drink. Get the support you need by giving Alcoholics Anonymous a ring. They're listed in the white section of your telephone directory. You have nothing to lose but your drinking problem.

In discussing this drinking problem, I have used male examples, but Carl tells me that alcoholism is not confined to men. He says that about one-third of their A.A. group is women. As he says, alcoholism is no respecter of age, sex, economic status, social position, or profession.

The undesirable habits I've covered in detail in this chapter are the main ones most people are bothered by. Others, such as a rotten temper, hostility and resentment toward others, jealousy, envy, laziness, and so on, can be solved by using the five general techniques I gave you back in the beginning of this chapter plus whatever other benefits you can list for yourself.

All you need do is just determine for yourself the benefits to be gained by breaking your bad habit, whatever it is, and then reprogram your subconscious mind with all those advantages that will be yours when you achieve your goal. Do that and you will be sure to be successful.

Now then—let's move on to the next chapter where I'll show you *How You Can Use the Mighty Powers of Your Subconscious Mind to Improve Your Health.*

How You Can Use the Mighty Powers of Your Subconscious Mind to Improve Your Health

11

Of course, when you get rid of your fears, your anxieties, and your worries as I showed you how to do in Chapter 9, your health will improve tremendously. And when you rid yourself of certain undesirable habits that I discussed in Chapter 10, your health will improve even more. However, there are still other active methods you can use to program your subconscious mind for even better health. I will discuss those methods and techniques with you in this chapter.

Admittedly, not all diseased conditions can be cured by using the powers of your subconscious mind, but, without exception, every single one of them can be helped. Amazingly, even such serious problems as cancer can be relieved. I'll tell you about two cases with which I am personally familiar, but first, I want to give you some of the....

TREMENDOUS HEALTH BENEFITS YOU CAN GAIN

In my own chiropractic practice I have found that some patients—whose vertebral subluxations had been corrected and whose diet and exercise regimens were adequate and well-rounded—still did

131

not achieve total health until I taught them how to program their subconscious minds with positive thoughts for further and final improvement. When I did that, here is how they responded:

They gained a new look of vigor and a change in the totality of consciousness and mental awareness. All of them seemed to visibly "brighten," as it were. And they all reported an enhanced performance, both physical and mental, in their everyday duties and activities.

This new keenness and vitality were obvious to everyone. Optimism, self-confidence, and a better outlook on life replaced their previous negative and pessimistic viewpoints. Downcast feelings were cast out. Where before there had been fatigue and that worn-out, tired feeling for no reason at all, there was now stamina, strength, and endurance.

They also found that even those minor illnesses and complaints—such as colds, occasional digestive upsets, miscellaneous aches and pains, which almost everyone suffers from now and then—were no longer as troublesome and irritating as they used to be.

They discovered that their improved mental attitudes led them to a higher degree of physical activity, including healthful exercise, such as walking, for it had now become pleasurable rather than drudgery, even for those who had previously literally cringed at the very thought of any physical exercise or exertion.

Even their sex lives were improved for many when they learned how to program their subconscious minds positively. A vigorous and continuing interest in sexual activity is a positive sign of good health. This interest should continue throughout one's adult life, even into the seventies and beyond, with physical performance to match this interest.

So let me ask you this now: Are you a person with just average, run-of-the-mill health? Is your weight far from what it should be, either over or under? Do you feel less vital and enthusiastic, more depressed and anxious, than you used to? Do you have angry or violent outbursts of temper, followed by periods of self-recrimination that make you feel as if you'd just like to crawl into a deep hole and stay there?

Do you avoid many social activities because you just don't feel "up to it," or claim that you're too tired and worn-out to go? Do you look back to your success of the past for comfort and consolation, rather than looking ahead for new challenges and more triumphs?

If any of these last two paragraphs are true for you, then this chapter will be of great benefit when you practice the techniques that

I'll give you here. If you will follow my recommendations fully and faithfully, in only 30 days or even less, you'll feel like a brand-new person who is filled with vigor and vitality, courage and enthusiasm, ready to take on the whole world, if need be. I know you will feel this way, for I have seen this "miracle" take place in countless numbers of my own patients.

TECHNIQUES YOU CAN USE TO GAIN THESE MAGNIFICENT BENEFITS

Now you shouldn't expect to eat nothing but junk foods, never exercise, not get the right amount of sleep, and then ask your subconscious mind to do it all for you. It will not work that way. You must cooperate by doing whatever you can to get your body into the best state of physical health possible. Then your subconscious mind can add the finishing touches for you. It's about like putting the frosting on the cake. Here, then, are....

Thirteen Tips on How to Help Your Subconscious Mind to Maintain Your Good Health

1. *Don't neglect your health completely* as so many people do. Take the same good care of your body as you do with that expensive automobile of yours. Your body is a much bigger and more valuable investment than your car is, although many people do not act as if that were so.

2. *Don't fuss about your health all the time.* Although it is important to safeguard your health and protect your body, don't become a fanatic about it. By that I mean don't go around listening for a knock in your motor. That's the best way of insuring that you will get sick.

3. *Don't get emotional, upset, and excited over every little thing that happens*, especially when it does not affect you or is no concern of yours. That's about like the preacher who constantly complains about the sinners who don't go to church and the sad state of the world instead of giving a positive message to those who are already there in his audience.

4. *Eat a healthful diet* with lots of fish and fowl and plenty of fresh fruits and vegetables. Don't load down your stomach with junk foods, manmade carbohydrates, or heavily spiced foods all the time. Your stomach is made out of living, sensitive tissue. It is not a cast-iron sink, so be kind to it.

5. *Get the proper amount of sleep your body needs.* Loss of sleep undermines your entire nervous system and makes you more susceptible, not only to emotional stress and strain, but also to a variety of contagious and infectious conditions.

6. *Relax* and give your body a chance to rest and recuperate throughout the day. Half an hour of quiet meditation will work wonders to improve your physical and mental, yes, even your spiritual condition.

7. *Exercise in moderation.* Walking, *not jogging,* one or two miles a day can help your lungs, your heart, and your circulation tremendously. Jogging can create more problems than it solves when your body isn't used to it.

8. *Do deep breathing exercises* at least once a day. Deep rhythmical breathing for several minutes brings in fresh oxygen, eliminates carbon dioxide and other waste products, and strengthens and renews your entire body.

9. *Don't be critical of others.* If you resent others and become angry with them, you'll be the one who gets ulcers, not them. Live and let live is a good motto to use. Just take inventory of your own defects, not someone else's, and you'll get along much better in life.

10. *Don't read books about disease all the time.* It's an old cliché that a little knowledge is a dangerous thing, but it is still true. It's perfectly fine to educate yourself and become well-informed, but I know from experience in my own practice that people who constantly read books about disease always seemed to have the symptoms of every ailment the author discussed. You'd be far better off to read books about health rather than disease when you're interested in improving your physical well-being.

11. *Don't discuss your ailments at great length* with anyone who will listen to you. You can be sure you're boring them, for chances are they don't have the slightest bit of interest in what you are saying. Not only that, you run the risk of making yourself sicker for you're only programming your subconscious mind negatively when you keep talking about your physical problems.

12. *Treat your body as the Holy Temple* the Bible says it is, and you'll be more apt to be in good health than not.

13. *Be cheerful and optimistic about life.* As it says in Proverbs 17:22, "A merry heart doeth good like a medicine: but a broken spirit drieth the bones." A more modern translation from the New English Bible of the last half of that sentence says that *low spirits sap a man's strength.* So be happy. It's good for both your heart and your stomach as well as

your general body health. My father always looked on the bright side of the worst situation. As he used to say, "When it starts raining inside the house, then I'll start worrying, but not until then."

How Your Imagination Can Work Against You to Cause Disease

Your imagination can keep you well or it can make you sick. It's all up to you. When your conscious mind programs your subconscious mind with the idea of good health, then you will be well. But if you program your subconscious mind with fear and thoughts of disease, then you will most certainly become sick. I have seen people receive a death sentence from the doctor, accept it, and go home to die. I have seen others receive the same death sentence, refuse to accept it, and outlive the doctor.

Let me show you now how your imagination can play tricks on you. Many a doctor gives a patient a placebo (usually a sugar pill) and gets the same results as if he had used the drug. Why? Because the person's conscious mind believed that he was getting the medicine he needed, and therefore, he programmed his subconscious mind with the idea that he would be cured. The end result was that he became well, all because he imagined that the placebo was the real thing.

A person under hypnosis can be told that an onion is an apple and he will eat it with relish without shedding a single tear. Or he can have a toothpick placed against his skin, be told that it is a burning match, and an actual blister will develop. Whatever the conscious mind believes to be true is transmitted to the subconscious mind. Then the subconscious mind accepts what has been programmed into it and acts accordingly.

Let me give you some facts and figures about how imagination can produce disease. A famous New Orleans medical clinic published a scientific paper recently that said that out of 500 patients suffering from gastro-intestinal problems, 74 percent were emotionally induced. The Yale University Out-Patient Medical Department said that 76 percent of patients coming to the clinic for treatment were suffering with emotionally induced illnesses.

In both cases, these people imagined themselves to be sick, so they developed all the symptoms of the disease. The symptoms, although imaginary in the beginning, did not remain that way. They became very real and caused actual physical problems.

Emotional problems and imaginary illnesses can cause pains in the neck, a lump in the throat, ulcer-like pains in the stomach, gallbladder pains, gas, dizziness, headaches, constipation, diarrhea, excessive fatigue, rapid pulse rate, palpitation of the heart, high blood pressure, excessive perspiration, on and on.

One of the best ways to control your emotions so you can avoid or prevent the conditions I have just mentioned is not to let your imagination run riot every time you have a pain somewhere. Remember that your subconscious mind cannot tell the difference between a real experience and one that is imagined. So don't imagine yourself to be sick. If you program your subconscious mind with the idea that you are ill, you can rest assured that you will be. Remember Job's experience. That is why it is so important that you use your imagination to program your subconscious mind with thoughts of good health, for quite literally, you will always become what you think about.

How Stress and Tension Can Cause Arthritis and Rheumatism

Some cases of arthritis can be caused by injury. For instance, professional football players often end up with arthritic and rheumatic knees and shoulders. Bad falls or accidents can also cause injury and result in arthritis. Usually, only one or two joints will be affected. A few cases of arthritis can be caused by localized infection. Again, normally only one or two joints will be involved.

However, by far most of the cases of arthritis or rheumatism I've treated in my practice are systemic in nature. That is to say, most of the joints in the body will be affected, although the pain and stiffness will always be more noticeable in one or two specific joints.

This kind of arthritis is caused by two basic factors which are always interrelated: *stress* and *tension*. Even when the arthritis has been caused by injury or infection, these two factors will compound the situation and make it even worse.

Stress and tension cause an undue expenditure of the body's energy. Let me give you a concrete example, like a trip to the dentist's office. Just the anticipation of the pain to come—*even if it never comes*—causes a person to tense up and grip the arms of the dentist's chair until the knuckles turn white. All the muscles in the body are tight, contracted, and strained. And when it's finally over, the patient almost crawls out of the chair, stiff and sore from the muscular, nervous, and mental stress, strain, and tension, often more tired than if he had done a full day's physical work.

Let me tell you exactly what physiological changes take place in the body when it is under stress, strain, and tension, as it is in that dentist's chair.

1. There is a sudden cessation of activity in the digestive tract. If a person has just eaten a full meal, the food now sits like a heavy lump of lead in the stomach.

2. Blood shifts from the abdominal organs to those essential to muscular exertion and activity; for example, the arms and legs.

3. There is an increase in the strength and speed of the contractions of the heart.

4. Extra red blood cells are discharged from the spleen into the circulation to carry more oxygen to the muscles.

5. There is deeper breathing and a dilation of the bronchial tubes that lead to the lungs so more oxygen can be taken into the body.

6. Blood sugar flows out of the liver to answer the body's increased energy demands.

These physiological changes prepare the body for *fight* or *flight*. Unfortunately, that is the exact situation so many of us find ourselves in all day long while at work. We are in a constant state of stress and tension from the time we get up in the morning until we go to bed at night.

Since most of us cannot run away from our environment to escape this stress and tension, we must stay and fight the problem, be that a frustrating job, a bitter career disappointment, a miserably mean boss, an unhappy marriage, or simply the never-ending daily and monthly bills.

Arthritis is on the rise because stress, strain, and tension are also increasing in our modern world. Prolonged nervous stress and emotional tension such as frustration, suppressed rage or anger, unhappiness, and depression are all "stressors" that can cause complete exhaustion—first, of the autonomic nervous system, and then, the adrenal glands. And this, in turn, leads to arthritis. It is a known scientific fact that *rheumatoid arthritis is almost always preceded by some severe nervous strain or emotional stress.*

A patient with arthritis will have an increase in pain when he is under some emotional strain that activates and exhausts his body's energy producing mechanism.

The key, then, to the prevention of arthritis, especially of the rheumatoid variety, is to avoid mental and emotional stress, strain, and tension. Program your subconscious mind with calm and peaceful thoughts. Complete relaxation through 30 minutes or more of quiet meditation can do wonders for you in preventing arthritis or rheumatism from ever gaining a foothold in your body.

But just in case you do contract the disease of arthritis, let me show you next what you can do about it.

How a Case of Severe Arthritis Was Cured with Laughter and Vitamin C

If you ever do come down with severe arthritis as Norman Cousins did, you can take hope from his case history. After a tense and stressful visit to Russia in 1964, Mr. Cousins was stricken with ankylosing spondylitis, a chronic, progressive arthritic disease of the spine that causes complete immobility.

His disease also migrated to the peripheral joints and he soon had great difficulty in moving his neck, arms, hands, legs, even his fingers. His jaws were almost locked and he lay in his hospital bed in excruciating agony. Mr. Cousins asked his doctor what his chances were for recovery. He was told that he had only one chance in 500. However, the specialist went on to say that he, himself, had never seen that one favorable case.

Mr. Cousins was taking 26 aspirin tablets a day as well as three phenylbutazone tablets (also a painkiller) four times daily. Allergy tests showed that he was hypersensitive to all of the medication he was receiving.

Now Norman Cousins, a former editor of the *Saturday Review of Literature*, is one of America's most distinguished journalists. He is both a fighter and a thinker. Since the odds were not in his favor with orthodox medical treatment, he resolved to get into the healing act himself and he did exactly that.

He decided to use vitamin C and laughter (which I will discuss in a few moments under *attitude*) to combat his condition. As I told you in the first part of this chapter, you cannot expect your subconscious mind to do everything for you. You must cooperate with it to get the job done. Proper nutrition is an integral part of good health. Since vitamin C falls into that category, I will discuss that with you first.

Vitamin C is known as the *antistress vitamin*. It stimulates the adrenal glands and increases the production of the hormone, *cortisone*, in the body. Cortisone is the body's own natural deterrent to rheumatism and arthritis.

Soldiers under the extreme stress and strain of combat in the battlefield always have drastically reduced vitamin C reserves in their bodies. This illustrates the importance of the antistress properties of vitamin C, and since stress was the cause of the problem Norman Cousins had, it was one of the wisest choices he could make.

Mr. Cousins started with 10 grams of vitamin C intravenously and increased the dosage until at the end of a week he was getting 25 grams daily. He was now completely off drugs and was enjoying prolonged periods of natural sleep without pain. Now let's discuss the second factor, *attitude*.

Attitude or mental outlook is the second factor that is so important in treating cases of arthritis and rheumatism. You cannot categorize physical types and say that a particular individual is more susceptible to arthritis because he is tall, short, thin, fat, light, or dark. But certain types of personalities are more apt to develop arthritis than others.

The arthritis-prone person is more likely to be a chronic worrier with a negative viewpoint. Norman Cousins recognized this fact in fighting his condition of ankylosing spondylitis. That's why he did everything he could to bring joy and laughter into his life to combat his illness. He had a film projector set up in his room so he could watch funny movies. His favorites were the Marx Brothers and Candid Camera classics.

He found that ten minutes of good hard laughter had an anesthetic effect that gave him no less than two hours of pain-free sleep. Laughter was also fighting the infection and the inflammation in his body. This was shown in laboratory tests of blood samples. Humor was proving to be a far better medicine than all the drugs that he had taken.

What was the final outcome of his case? Complete and total health was restored for Mr. Cousins with laughter and vitamin C. He went back to playing tennis and—after his manual dexterity was restored—enjoying his favorite melodies on the organ. He also returned full-time to his position as editor with the *Saturday Review*.

I ask all my patients with arthritis and rheumatism, not only to take large amounts of vitamin C, but also to develop a positive, optimistic outlook on life and to enjoy a good, hearty belly laugh every day. I recommend that you do the same even if you don't have arthritis or rheumatism. Maybe you can't set up a movie projector in your living room to watch the Marx Brothers or Candid Camera as Norman Cousins did. But you can devise your own system to bring joy and happiness into your life.

Sure, it's hard to laugh and be joyful when you are in pain and you hurt, either physically or mentally. But it can be done. Let me give you a specific example to prove that point.

I once had a patient, Mrs. B., who was troubled with chronic indigestion, rheumatoid arthritis, high blood pressure, and palpitation of the heart, all caused by emotional and mental stress, strain, and tension.

You see, Mrs. B. had a family of four children and a husband who had been drunk nearly every day of their married life. She worked as a clerk in a department store to support the family.

This poor woman and her children were submerged in a sea of misery, shame, and unhappiness because of her husband's behavior. Every possible approach had been tried to help him break his drinking habit, but nothing had worked.

One day, after long months of counseling from me, Mrs. B. made the most important decision of her life. She resolved not to torture herself anymore about her husband's drinking problem. "I will take care of him," she told me, "but I am not going to worry myself sick over him any longer as I have done in the past. I am going to devote all my energies from now on to making my life and the lives of my children as happy as possible under these trying circumstances."

In only a few short months, Mrs. B's changed attitude had given her much better mental and physical health. She still had her problem—her husband had not stopped drinking—but she was determined to be joyful and happy anyway.

If she could laugh and be happy in the middle of such an unhappy and trying situation as that, then I'll wager that you can be happy and joyful and laugh, too.

If rheumatism or arthritis is your problem, and you would like to know more about how it can be relieved, I would suggest you get a copy of my Special Report entitled *A Doctor's Proven New Way to Conquer Rheumatism and Arthritis*. It is published by Parker Publishing Company, West Nyack, New York, 10994. Just drop them a line and ask for either a copy of the report (they'll send it to you and bill you later) or an informational brochure on the report.

How Even Cancer Can Be Helped with the Mighty Power of the Subconscious Mind

A neighbor of mine, a retired Marine Corps colonel, developed cancer of the liver over seven years ago. Colonel J. went to Keesler Air Force Base Hospital in Biloxi, Mississippi for treatment. There he was told to get his earthly affairs in order for he had less than six months to live.

But the colonel was a fighter and he refused to accept the doctor's verdict of death. He came home and started his own cancer treatment program. His regimen consisted of massive amounts of vitamin C and E and daily meditation periods where he used mental pictography to visualize his cancer cells being eaten by his body's white blood cells.

He has gone back to the hospital in Mississippi every three months for the past seven years for examination. During all this time, although the cancer did not regress, neither did it grow any larger. After the last examination a few weeks ago, Colonel J. came home thrilled and happy beyond words. For the first time in more than seven years the cancer appeared to be smaller on the x-ray films and his doctors told him it was evidently shrinking and disappearing. Although it is too early to say that the colonel is completely cured, still the cancer is smaller and he has already lived more than six and a half years longer than doctors told him that he would.

Another case of treatment of cancer by visualization therapy is that of a nine-year-old boy. Gregory had a malignant tumor involving much of the right side of the brain. After a full course of radiation therapy, he was no better. The cancer was still growing and the doctors were calling his case a medical treatment failure.

"They all expected him to die," says Dr. Patricia Norris, the clinical director of the Biofeedback and Psychophysiology Center at the Menninger Foundation in Topeka, Kansas. But instead of taking him home to die, Gregory's parents brought him to Dr. Norris for help. Using a technique called "visualization therapy," Gregory was taught to form a mental picture of his cancer.

It became a space battle in his mind. His disease-fighting white blood cells became a deadly fighter squadron. Gregory was the squadron leader. Doctor Norris was ground control, guiding and supporting him through his mental battle for his life. After one year of waging mental war against his tumor, it was gone. Today, five years later, at the age of 14, Gregory is still cancer-free.

Scientific studies linking the mind to physical health and disease are now a matter of exciting research. Investigators have found that negative emotions and severe stress can cause the development of a variety of diseases, including cancer, while positive thoughts, usually achieved through meditation, can heal a long list of health problems.

Research in this new field, called *psychoneuroimmunology*, a term defining the interrelationship between mind, body, and the body's immune system, is causing doctors to rethink one of medicine's time-honored tenets that the mind and the body are distinct and separate entities.

Among the findings leading to this reappraisal are studies showing that (a) severe stress, such as a spouse's death or the diagnosis of cancer, can impair immune system function, (b) people with emotional short circuits that keep them from experiencing emotions or fantasies are an increased risk for a variety of diseases, including cancer, (c) severe depression can prevent white blood cells from fighting off disease in the body.

While she is still hesitant to endorse the kind of visualization therapy she used with Gregory as a solitary weapon against cancer, Dr. Norris does feel it can play an important role in treatment, for she says she has seen it work time after time.

What Dr. Norris and others have seen clinically may now have been explained scientifically by a group of researchers at George Washington University School of Medicine. They have been studying patients who practice visualization or mental imagery.

These researchers have found that mental imagery or visualization causes an increase in a certain body chemical known as *thymosin alpha-1*. This body chemical causes an increase in the number and potency of certain white blood cells that attack and destroy cancer cells.

These two examples vividly demonstrate the power of the body's subconscious mind. When programmed properly, as in these two cases of mental imagery or visualization, it will go all out to help a person fight disease, no matter what that disease is.

How Other Health Problems Can Be Relieved by Eliminating Stress and Tension

1. *Asthma is an ailment that handicaps many people.* A bad asthmatic attack is a terrifying experience and can even result in death. Drugs can help the asthmatic to breathe and control the condition, but they will not cure the asthma itself.

Emotional factors, such as stress and tension, can not only bring on an asthmatic attack, but they can also intensify it. The basic physiology of asthma is that the patient is unable to expel the air that has been breathed in. Muscular tension in the tissues around the lung sacs blocks breathing out. If this tension can be relieved, then breathing will become normal again. Drugs, if inhaled, tend to open up the air sacs and reduce the muscle tension. The fear of an attack or fear of any sort will cause an asthmatic spasm to start.

Hypnotism has been very useful in treating asthma. Although I am not a professional hypnotist, I have been able to help my asthmatic patients by teaching them the art of meditation. Meditation is in a way a kind of self-hypnotism and when the patient relaxes, his asthma is immediately improved. Daily meditation used consistently over a period of time can alleviate the asthmatic condition together.

2. *Allergies can be either physical or mental or both.* Some allergies, hay fever, for example, are physical and caused by pollens. The biggest culprit of all is ragweed. However, even physical allergies can be intensified by improper programming of the subconscious mind.

When the hay fever season arrives, the allergy victim will start sneezing, his eyes will water, and he will have all the typical symptoms of his allergy, *even if he has not yet been exposed to the pollen.* He has programmed his subconscious mind to react when the hay fever season arrives, and it does so automatically. Let me give you a classic example of how your imagination can fool you.

A certain patient of mine was allergic to roses. A friend had given me a rose made out of velvet that was so lifelike you could not tell it was artificial unless you felt the petals of the flower. When this allergic patient entered my office one day, he saw the artificial rose on my receptionist's desk and promptly began to sneeze and suffer an allergic respiratory attack.

My receptionist then handed him the rose and called his attention to the fact that it was artificial, not real. His allergic attack immediately ended.

3. *High blood pressure can be lowered permanently with consistent meditation.* I always asked all my patients with high blood pressure problems to meditate no less than twice daily. I found that after a month or so of meditation therapy, the systolic (top) readings could be reduced as much as 25 points and the diastolic (bottom) as much as 15. For example, I have seen the systolic drop from 190 down to 165 and the diastolic go from 95 to 80. These readings were not taken during actual meditation, but when the patient came to my office for a routine visit.

Why does meditation cause a reduction in blood pressure? Well, first of all, the patient is getting rid of stress and tension by relaxing. The relaxation during meditation also causes the body to produce its own internal natural "beta blockers." Synthetic beta blockers are the drugs used to medically treat patients with hypertension or high blood pressure.

I am not suggesting that you should put off having your blood pressure checked or that you should stop taking the medication prescribed by your doctor when you start using meditation. But you can help yourself and improve your health by helping to lower your blood pressure naturally.

4. *How you can get rid of constipation.* Of every 10 patients I saw, at lest six or seven were troubled by constipation. It seems to be a national malady, no doubt brought on by a diet rich in junk foods and manmade carbohydrates. Lower colon spasm can be relieved by meditation and relaxation.

You can help yourself to get rid of constipation, not only by relaxation and meditation, but also by programming your subconscious mind to move your bowels at a specific time of the day every single day.

First of all, program your subconscious mind to *expect* a normal bowel movement. I have found that most of my patients with chronic constipation problems never expected to have a normal bowel movement. In this negative frame of mind, when the person does try to go to the bathroom, the law of reversed effect goes into operation and there is naturally no result.

So your first step is to program your subconscious mind to expect a normal bowel movement. You can help this programming simply by sitting on the stool expectantly, at whatever time you have selected that best fits your schedule.

I, myself, have programmed my subconscious mind to cause my body to have a normal BM right after my first cup of coffee in the morning. Does that work? It most certainly does. My subconscious mind is so well programmed, I dare not be too far away from the bathroom when I finish that first cup of coffee if I want to prevent a disaster.

You can also help your body's digestive system by eating plenty of high-fiber foods, lots of fresh fruits and vegetables, and by avoiding canned and packaged foods that contain large amounts of manmade sugars. Remember, as I have said before, you cannot expect your subconscious mind to do everything for you. You must be its partner and cooperate with it if you want total good health.

How the Subconscious Mind Helped Control Excessive Bleeding During a Serious Operation

One of my neighbors had a serious abdominal operation some time ago. He was familiar with my methods and techniques, so he programmed his subconscious mind to prevent excessive bleeding during his operation.

The surgical nurse was also familiar with programming of the subconscious mind to control body functions, so as he was dropping off under the anesthetic, she kept whispering in his ear, "You will not bleed . . . you will not bleed . . . you will not bleed."

As a result he did not bleed excessively. In fact, he lost so little blood, no transfusion was required. Usually, a blood transfusion is standard practice during this particular kind of operation. His surgeon was amazed at how little blood was lost. He later told my friend he had never before performed this operation without the patient being given a transfusion.

Examples of Emotionally Induced Illnesses Solved by a Change in Attitude

I have had patients who had all their spinal subluxations corrected, who were on an excellent diet and an adequate exercise program, yet who failed to respond completely and still did not feel entirely well.

Such cases taught me to expand my case history of a patient to include such questions as, "Is anyone causing you a problem in life? Do you hate, despise, or resent some individual? You don't have to name names. Just tell me if someone is bothering you, and, if so, in what way?"

When I asked questions like these, I began to get answers that gave me an insight into what was really wrong with the patient. Let me give you a few brief examples:

1. One man was worried about cancer of the rectum, although a proctologist had given him a complete exam and discovered nothing wrong. Yet his pain and discomfort persisted. Careful questioning revealed that his employer was the source of his trouble. His exact words to me and I quote were, "My boss gives me a pain in the ass!"

When I explained to him that the way he was thinking about his boss was actually programming his subconscious mind to cause him rectal pain and discomfort, he was able to overcome his problem by a change in attitude and reprogramming of his subconscious mind.

2. Another patient, a woman, was troubled with shooting pains in the neck. Cervical adjustments had lined up her neck vertebrae properly and x-rays proved that. Yet her pains continued. Careful questioning of her revealed the true cause of her problem. As she put it, a certain person gave her a "big pain in the neck." Just as with the previ-

ous patient, an explanation of what she was doing to herself enabled her to solve her problem.

3. Another individual was troubled with stomach cramps, indigestion, diarrhea, and occasional vomiting, all without apparent reason. The cause? Someone was making him "sick to his stomach." Just as with the others, the case was easily resolved when the patient understood how he was programming his subconscious mind improperly and causing his own problem.

I could give you many other examples, but these three should be enough for you to understand how physical problems can be caused by improper attitudes and negative programming of your subconscious mind. If you have some condition that your doctor has not been able to solve, check yourself out and see if you are not creating your own problem by how and what you are thinking that programs your subconscious mind improperly. Do that and you may be well able to heal yourself.

How to Handle Those Incurable Conditions

Arms, legs, eyes, and so on lost through accident or operations are not replaceable. I have yet to see a person grow a new eye, arm, or leg with the power of the subconscious mind. However, the correct attitude will help you program your subconscious mind properly so you can learn to accept and manage your own particular situation, no matter how difficult it is, or what it happens to be.

Let me give you three quick examples of this:

1. Chuck, a man who was born deaf, has learned to speak so he can be understood. He can carry on a conversation for he has also learned to read lips. He is married, and the father of two children. He drives his own car and holds down a full-time position in an electronics factory as a quality control inspector. Even though he has never heard a single sound in all his life, Chuck has accomplished all this because of his positive attitude and his refusal to accept defeat. As a result, he has succeeded where others would have failed completely.

2. Jed B., is a legless amputee and is confined to a wheelchair as a result of war wounds. He is the service officer of the local DAV. At the last meeting, officers were elected for the new year. Jed was re-elected to his post as service officer. After the election, the new officers were asked to stand so they could be recognized by all.

"Jed, stand up and be recognized," the commander said jokingly.

"You think I can't?" Jed retorted with a smile, and he raised himself up with his arms and stood in his wheelchair seat on the stumps of his legs.

Jed, too, has refused to accept defeat, and as a result, life to him is well worthwhile in spite of his handicap. By devoting his life to helping others, he has been able to forget his own problems.

3. My own wife has been a victim of multiple sclerosis for more than 30 years. The disease has completely destroyed her sense of balance and she cannot stand up unless she has something to hold onto. She gets around the house in an electric three wheeled go-cart. She still cooks our meals and is active in church and social work. She keeps the circulation and muscle tone in her legs by riding a stationary bicycle and using a rowing machine every day.

Her attitude about all this? The best answer I can give you is that her friends all call her "Smiley." Does that answer your question?

I could not possibly cover all the physical ailments or diseases that can be improved or healed with the mighty powers of your subconscious mind. If I were to attempt to do that, this chapter would have quickly become a book

However, you can easily help yourself, no matter what your illness is, for the methods used to properly program your subconscious mind will be exactly the same as those that I have described in this chapter.

Now let's get on to Chapter 12, where I'll show you how you can use the hidden power of your subconscious mind to improve your personal relationships with others.

How to Use the Hidden Power of Your Subconscious Mind to Improve Your Personal Relationships with People

12

YOUR PERSONALITY

Your relationships with others will depend entirely upon your personality. And your total personality depends completely upon how you have programmed your subconscious mind. For example, if you have contaminated your subconscious mind with negative thoughts of hate, envy, resentment, anger, jealousy, bitterness, and the like, that is exactly the kind of person you are going to be and the sort of personality you will project to others.

However, even if this has happened, your negative personality can be changed completely. All you need do is reprogram your subconscious mind with positive thoughts of tolerance and patience, love and kindness, and your entire life can be turned around, literally overnight.

If you will remember, I have said before that unless you give your subconscious mind a goal to shoot for, it will not work for you. In this particular situation, your specific goal should be to improve your relationships with others: your family, your friends, your neighbors, and your business associates.

Definition of a "True" Friend

Now most of us feel lucky if we can count our *true* friends on the fingers of one hand. Exactly what is a "true" friend? Well, my own definition of a true friend is one who will accept me just as I am with all my faults and frailties and still love me in spite of those character defects. A real friend's attitude toward me, then, could best be expressed by this simple statement:

I like you *because* . . . but I love you *in spite of* . . .

That's the kind of true friend I'm talking about. Since friends are won or lost, primarily by what you do and say, then your language—not only what you say but also how you say it—becomes extremely significant. Not only that, what you say and how you say it will be completely dependent on how you program your subconscious mind. Remember that output always equals input.

I want to use the rest of this chapter to give you the techniques you can use to gain your goal of improving your personal relationships with people, both inside and outside your own family. When you do that,

YOU'LL GAIN THESE SIX TERRIFIC BENEFITS

1. A true friend will be one who sticks by you when the going gets rough. He'll not desert you at the first sign of trouble. You can depend upon his wholehearted support to see you through your tough times.

2. A true friend will trust you and have complete confidence in you, no matter what. As the old saying goes, "Never explain what you say or do to anyone. Your friends don't need it and your enemies won't believe it." You don't have to prove yourself to a real friend to hold his loyal friendship.

3. No matter what you say or do, a true friend will accept you just as you are. He'll not criticize you for your faults and character defects. He may not like them, of course, but he will tolerate them with kindness while praising your good points and fine qualities to others.

4. When you gain a person's friendship, you'll also gain his re-

spect. True friends will respect you, your decisions, and your actions. They'll willingly and gladly do whatever they can to help you.

5. A true friend will never speak disparagingly about you. Not only that, he will do everything he can to squelch rumors or gossip that degrades you or blackens your reputation. He'll never say anything behind your back that he would not say to you face-to-face.

6. As you learn the how-to of making close friends, you'll become an expert in the art of human relations, for making and keeping friends requires tact, diplomacy, and skill.

Techniques You Can Use to Gain These Terrific Benefits

Why you must first give if you want to get

If you are kind to others, they will be kind to you. If you are courteous to others, they will be courteous to you. And if you are friendly to others, then they will also be friendly to you. Your actions are always reflected to you from the other person, as if you were looking in a mirror.

So the first point to remember about making good friends is simply this: *If you want to get, then you must first give of yourself.* It is absolutely impossible to give of yourself to someone else and get nothing in return.

Now a petty, nearsighted person often refuses to give of himself because he cannot see how or where he is going to profit by so doing. Therefore, he gets nothing back because he gave nothing away. So you see, the maxim still holds true, even in his case, for he got back exactly what he gave away: *nothing*.

But the farsighted person gives of himself without any thought of return and gains friends because of that. Let me give you an example now so you can see for yourself how well this technique can work for you.

Pete Randall is a cookie salesman out of Des Moines who calls upon retail merchants in north-central Iowa. Pete's cookies are good, but they are really no better than half a dozen other competing brands. Yet Pete outsells his competition all the time. How does he do that? *By giving of himself and taking the time to help the grocer sell his products.*

"A small town grocer doesn't have the backing that big chain stores do for floor display and advertising," Pete says. "Nor does he have the manpower to help him. If he's going to get it done, he has to do it himself or get his wife to help him.

"Now you don't walk into a man's place of business and tell him how to run things. It rubs him the wrong way and you could easily lose a customer. So I wait until the time is just right, when he either asks for help or when I find him right in the middle of putting up a cookie advertising display. Then I pitch right in and help him.

"I remember a store in Eagle Grove, the So-Lo Market, where I helped the owner put up a display for one of my cookie competitors. Next time around, he wanted me to help him again, for he had done a booming business with that display, but this time he wanted to do it with my cookies.

"Now he pushes my brand all the time, and, in return, I bring him all sorts of suggestions on displays and advertising on everything from brushes and brooms to yams and yogurt.

"In 90 percent of the stores I service, my cookies outsell every competing brand—just because the owners push my line instead of the others. I help them whenever I can and in return, they go all-out for me."

So the first rule for making valuable friends is to first give of yourself to the other person. Do everything in your power to increase the success and happiness of the other individual. That's exactly what Pete does. You've seen how he profits by so doing. You will profit, too, by having more true friends than you ever thought possible when you use this same technique.

You'll also profit in other ways as well. When you build your friendships on the basis of benefit, profit, and success for others, you'll find that they will be glad to help you by doing whatever they can to advance your interests, too.

How to build your friendships on a solid foundation

Now that you know and understand the first law of making valuable friends, I want to show you a simple way to put this principle of giving of yourself to others to work. I know you might feel you are not in a position to help others as Pete Randall does, but you don't have to be.

You can use this method to win friends, no matter who they are—your boss, your employees, your associates at work or in church or your social groups, it matters not. All you need do is *praise the other person for what he has done.*

To be praised is a basic human desire. We all want to be told how great we are and what a good job we've done. Even the United States

Army found that praise works far better than criticism in getting soldiers to do a better job. When soldiers were praised for their efforts, nine out of ten did a better job the next time around. But when they were criticized, only three out of ten did a better job the next time.

Praise a person and you'll win his loyal friendship. He'll love you for it. So tell him what a magnificent job he's doing . . . how you couldn't get along without him . . . how happy you are that he is your friend.

Be generous with your praise. Pass it around freely. The supply is limited only by you. Don't be stingy about passing out bouquets; they cost you nothing. Above all, don't act as if you expected something in return for your praise. Don't pay a person a compliment as if you wanted a receipt for it.

Not only does praise feed a person's ego and fulfill his desire to be more important, but it also satisfies nine more of the 14 basic needs and desires every one of us has. Let me list those nine for you here so you can see for yourself what a valuable tool praise can be in winning and holding a friendship for you.

1. Recognition of efforts, reassurance of worth.
2. Approval and acceptance by others.
3. The accomplishment or achievement of something worthwhile.
4. A sense of roots, a sense of belonging, a feeling of being both needed and wanted.
5. A sense of self-esteem, dignity, and self-respect.
6. The desire to win, to be first, to excel.
7. Love and friendship.
8. Emotional security.
9. A sense of personal power.

When you can fulfill nine of a person's 14 basic desires just by praising him, then it makes good sense to do so. You can be sure he'll want to be your friend when he gets treatment like this from you.

Specific ways you can use praise to gain a person's friendship

In the happiest marriages, husbands and wives are friends as well as lovers. If you are the husband, you can praise your wife in any number of ways to win her friendship. For instance, if your morning coffee is good, tell her so. If it isn't good, tell her it is anyway. This is one time when a tiny white lie is permissible.

Be generous with your praise. Don't wait until she does something big or unusual to praise her for. Praise her for her excellent cooking, her magnificent housekeeping, her beautiful appearance, her gorgeous hair-do. And don't forget to thank her for what she does for you. That is also praise. The two simple words, "Thank you," can be a real morale booster to a tired and worn-out housewife.

If you are the wife and you want your husband to be successful in his work, then you can help him by the simple act of praising him for what he does. Praise builds his self-confidence and helps him do a better job. Your praise can send him off each morning filled with the confidence that he can solve any problem that comes his way.

How to use praise instead of flattery

Always be sure to use praise, not flattery, to build strong and enduring friendships. To flatter a person means to praise him far beyond what is true or to praise him insincerely. The dictionary says flattery is praise that is usually untrue or overstated. In other words, to flatter is simply to lie. To be sincere means to be genuine and honest, free from all pretense and deceit.

Flattery is as phony as a three-dollar bill. People can always spot your phoniness and see through you immediately.

There is an extremely easy way for you to determine whether you are praising a person sincerely or whether you are just flattering him. Flattery praises a person for what he *is*, not for what he *does*. Praise congratulates a person for what he *does*, not for what he *is*. Let me show you the difference now between these two by the following four brief examples:

FLATTERY: Reverend, you are the nicest preacher we have ever had in our church.

PRAISE: That was an inspiring sermon you gave this morning. We can always use more like that.

FLATTERY: Tom, you're the best salesman we have in the entire company.

PRAISE: Congratulations, Tom. You had the most sales in the entire district last month. That's an outstanding record. Thanks a lot for your excellent work. I really do appreciate it.

FLATTERY: George, you're the smartest worker in the whole plant.

PRAISE: George, that suggestion of yours was an outstanding idea. It's going to save us a lot of time and unnecessary steps. Thanks a million for your help.

FLATTERY: Miss Jones, you're really the most beautiful typist in the company.

PRAISE: Miss Jones, your typing is absolutely superb. I have no hesitancy about signing my correspondence now. I really do appreciate your excellent work. Thanks a lot.

See the difference here? Flattery is vague, ill-defined, and usually confusing. It leaves the flattered person wondering *Why? How? When? In what way?* He doesn't know what he has actually done to deserve the praise, so he is in no position to repeat his performance. Flattery does nothing to help the person improve his work methods.

And in the case of Miss Jones, telling her she's the most beautiful typist in the company is really confusing. She's left wondering if the boss is talking about her typing skills, or if he's getting ready to make a pass at her.

Genuine praise does not create confusion. Not only that, when you praise a person for *what* he does, not for what he *is*, you are forced to find something to praise him for. That makes you look for his good points rather than his weak ones. Genuine praise requires thought, energy, and effort on your part, but it is well worth it in the long run. Praise others and you will be able to build many strong and enduring friendships.

How to be well-liked by everyone

If you want to know the secret of being liked by everyone wherever you go, then learn to *give your wholehearted* attention to the other person. Every individual in this whole wide world, from the smallest baby to the oldest man or woman, wants the attention of others. He wants to be listened to, he wants to be heard. He wants others to listen to his ideas, his opinions, his suggestions, and his recommendations. He has a deep and burning desire—yes, even an insatiable craving—to be important, to be great, to be famous. And one of the best methods you can use to make a person feel important is to pay attention to him and to what he says.

Just for instance, take the person who has never had his picture in the paper since his high school graduation. Why, he'll jump at the chance when it's offered to him. That's why people always wave when the TV camera swings their way at a football or baseball game. It's an automatic reaction to gain attention and feel important.

Let me explain that last statement to you more fully. You see, our actions to attract another person's attention are simply the outward manifestations of our inner desires for importance. We yearn for attention. We want our ideas and opinions to be heard. The desire for attention is present in every single one of us. If you think not, let me ask you this: Have you ever been snubbed by a haughty waiter, left standing on a corner by an independent bus driver, or completely ignored by a government bureaucrat or store clerk? How did you feel? Now you know what I'm driving at, don't you.

Psychologists, psychiatrists, ministers, criminologists, management consultants, marriage counselors, all these experts in this art of human relations have come to one simple conclusion. That is, if you want to be well liked by others, then you must learn to give your wholehearted attention to the other person. It is one of the surest ways of establishing solid friendly relationships with other people.

This technique of how to be well-liked by others will work miracles for you, not only with people outside your immediate family, but also with your spouse and your children. Let me give you a couple of brief examples of this:

1. *How to Pay Attention to Your Wife.*

You don't have to send your wife flowers or candy every day or buy her expensive gifts all the time to show her how much you love and appreciate her. My technique will cost you absolutely nothing and it's even more effective. I know a couple who've been happily married for more than 40 years now, and I know for a fact that this man doesn't give his wife any presents except on three really important occasions: her birthday, their anniversary, and Christmas.

"What's your secret, Sam?" I asked him one day.

"Very simple, Jim," he said. "I always pay attention to my wife. I let her know by my actions every day that I know she's around. I still say *please* and *thank you* even after all these years. So does she; sort of builds a mutual respect between us. And I never get up from the table without saying, 'Thanks, honey; that was a terrific meal,' or 'Thanks a lot, dear; you're sure a wonderful cook.'

"Or when we pass each other in the house, I reach out and touch her hand. Or I bring her a glass of water when she's watching TV in the evening. Or a cup of tea in the afternoon while she's sewing or reading. What if she doesn't want it, you say. What if she's not thirsty? Don't worry about that. She'll drink it anyway just to show her appreciation for my giving her my wholehearted attention. If you don't believe that works, try it on your own wife. You'll soon see for yourself how much she appreciates it."

I know these might sound like tiny, inconsequential things to you at first. But just as Sam says, they serve as proof positive to your wife that you still love her and that you still appreciate her. So if you want to maintain a harmonious relationship and a pleasant atmosphere in your home, then all you need do is give your wholehearted attention to your wife, too.

You'll be mighty happy when you do. When you do these little things for her, your own benefits will multiply. You'll never want for a clean shirt, you'll never put on a pair of unpressed pants, or you'll never sit down to a cold supper.

Your wife will love all those *little inconsequential, unimportant extras* and she'll want to make sure they keep coming. And if you're the wife, this technique will work in reverse, for you can use it on your husband, too.

There are very few magic words or phrases, but as you can see in the example of Sam and his wife, *please* and *thank you* are two of them. Use them constantly, for they will work magic for you in your relationships with others.

I know that to be a fact, for there is a grocery store less than three blocks from my house, but I never go there. The check-out clerks are always sour-faced and don't know how to say "Thank you." So I drive nearly three miles to a different supermarket simply because the people there are friendly and courteous and never fail to say "Thanks." Who says you can't mix friendship and business?

2. *How to Use This Technique on Your Children, Too.*

If you have been having disciplinary problems with your children, this technique of paying attention to them will go a long way toward solving them. I know for I raised three of my own.

Many parents make the mistake of not paying attention to their children. They don't want to be bothered with them or with their problems. But children need and want attention just as much as grownups do, sometimes even more.

Now it doesn't take a lot of extra effort to give your children that extra attention they need so much. It just takes time. Ask them to play with you. Don't wait for them to ask you. Perhaps a game of pool, ping-pong, cards, chess, checkers, monopoly—whatever you have in your home.

Larry, my youngest son, and I used to battle it out with a cribbage board in front of the fireplace on many a stormy winter night when we lived in the north. In the summer, you had to get in line to play ping-pong in the garage.

So learn to play with your children; pay attention to them. It will improve all of your family relationships. Your kids will learn to like you as well as love you. You'll be not only their parents, but also you'll become their friends, and that's ever so important. A good healthy game of ping-pong in the garage with your teenage son or daughter will do more to reduce that generation gap than all the lectures you can give them in the back bedroom.

How to become genuinely interested in other people

I know of no faster way on earth of driving people away from you and becoming extremely unpopular with everyone than to continually talk about yourself and your own accomplishments. Not even your best friends can put up with your never-ending stories of how important you are. Even they will reach the limits of their endurance. So a big secret of making and keeping friends is to *forget yourself completely and become genuinely interested in other people.*

If you believe you can be well-liked, highly popular, and win friends by getting them interested in you and your affairs, then I must tell you quite bluntly, you are dead wrong. The only way you can ever win lasting friends is to become truly interested in people and in their problems.

The selfish person who has no interest in his fellow human being and his problems always has the greatest difficulties in life and ends up causing the most harm, not only to others, but also to himself. That individual is bound to fail unless he changes his basic selfish attitude toward people. If you do by some rare chance happen to find yourself in that rut, here are two giant steps you can take to get out of it so you can become genuinely interested in others:

1. Forget yourself completely.
2. Think that other people are important.

How to forget yourself completely

All of us are self-centered almost all the time. To me—the world revolves around me. But as far as you are concerned—it revolves around you. Most of us are busily trying to impress someone. We are constantly seeking the spotlight. We continually want to be in the center of the stage. Most of our waking moments are spent in trying to achieve status of some sort.

But if you want to be well-liked and make friends with others, you must learn to forget yourself completely. You can do that easily when you give service of some sort to others. If you want to win the hearts and minds of people, then you must be willing to help them in any way you can.

To be able to do this with sincerity means you'll have to place more emphasis on what they want than upon what you want. And you will need an attitude of complete unselfishness to do that.

I know this much for sure. If you are truly sincere, if you will become genuinely interested in helping others, you will have more friends than you can ever count. Everybody will be able to say a good word for you. You will be well-liked and have friends wherever you go.

How to think that other people are important

This is the second step I mentioned that you can use to become genuinely interested in others. Jesus once said, "Believe that you have got it and you shall have it." The same principle applies here. In other words, all you need do to think that other people are important is just to *pretend that they are and they will be.*

Simply tell yourself once and for all that other people and their interests are more important to them than you and your interests are. When you adopt this attitude and practice it sincerely, it will come through as clear as a bell to the other person. You won't have to put on a phony face and butter him up to win his friendship.

With this new approach you can stop looking for gimmicks to become well-liked and win friends. You won't need any gimmicks for you'll have put your dealings with others on a firm, sound, sincere, and honest basis. Sincerity and honesty are better than a gimmick any day of the week, for you can't make a person feel important if deep down inside you really feel he's a worthless nobody.

The beauty of this method is you no longer need participate in the games people play to impress each other. All you need do to make this technique work is just to think that the other person is important and then treat him that way. Pretend that it is so, and it will be.

Why you should accept a person exactly as he or she is

To accept a person exactly as he or she is provides not only the sound basis for a solid friendship, but it is also one of the secrets of a happy and successful marriage.

If you want to be able to accept people exactly as they are, then concentrate on their good points and overlook their defects. The person doesn't live who's achieved perfection. To the best of my knowledge, only one person ever lived who was perfect and He was crucified for it.

Never Criticize a Person if you want to be able to accept him exactly as he or she is. Criticism is a quick way to destroy a friendship. When you tell a person that he is wrong or that he shouldn't do this or that, his feathers are immediately ruffled, he goes on the defensive at once, and he resents your comments, no matter how well intentioned they might have been. Let me give you an example of how to avoid criticizing someone even when you know that they're wrong.

Last year I was on the Chamber of Commerce committee that was responsible for soliciting money from business people to buy toys for poor children at Christmas time.

Gene Baxter and I went together on most occasions, feeling it was easier to collect with two people rather than with only one. One old grumpy merchant complained loudly about giving. "I don't believe in charity," he said. "Nobody ever gave me anything. I earned it all myself. Besides, the Bible says, 'God helps those who help themselves.' "

"I agree with you," I said, "but we're not asking for much. Besides, it's the children we want to help. After all, they're not old enough to help themselves as you so wisely suggest."

He relented then, and after we left with his check in hand, Gene said, "Jim, I've never heard that Bible quotation before, have you?"

"No, Gene, I haven't," I said, "because it doesn't come from the Bible. But if we had told him he was wrong, we wouldn't have his check for the children, now would we?"

There is no point in telling a person that he's wrong just to show him that he's wrong. When you do that, you are criticizing him and criticism destroys friendships. Not only that, it creates enemies. And life is too short to have enemies. Even one is one too many.

How to avoid arguments and disagreements at all costs

One of the best ways to keep out of arguments is to do as I have just suggested: never criticize the other person. But there will be times when a person becomes angry with you for one reason or another, usually because of something he thinks you've said or done, even though you haven't. Here's the best way to handle that kind of situation.

When a person becomes angry with you, you have your choice of doing one of two things. You can retaliate, get mad, and fight back, or you can do exactly the opposite—appease his anger.

If you fight back—which is exactly what the other person expects you to do—you will lose complete control of the situation and only make matters worse. You will accomplish absolutely nothing by losing your temper, too.

What happens, then, if you don't fight back? Does that mean the other person automatically wins? Of course not. The only time you can be really sure of winning is when you don't lose your temper and retaliate. It always takes two to make a fight. When you refuse to become angry, then the other person's anger simply has to burn itself out.

Verne Nichols, a friend of mine, tells me he handles arguments and disagreements this way:

"I have a neighbor with a short fuse who flies off the handle at the slightest provocation," Verne says. "Used to be when he came over raising the dickens about something, I'd get mad, yell back, and we'd get nowhere. We fought like crazy until I learned how to handle his temper tantrums. Now when he gets upset or angry about something, I stay calm instead of flying off into a great rage. When I refuse to fight, he realizes he might just as well cuss out a tree or a bush, so he throws in the towel and gives up."

The best way, then, to turn off a person's anger immediately and keep out of a disagreement or argument with him is to respond in a kind and friendly manner. Remain calm and say nothing for a few moments until he has drained himself emotionally.

Then answer him quietly and softly, for as the Bible says, "A soft answer turneth away wrath," and that is ever so true. If you use a soft, quiet tone of voice, it will not only calm down the other person, but also it will keep you from getting angry as well.

When you refuse to fight back, when you speak softly, the angry person suddenly realizes that he's the only one shouting. This embarrasses him and makes him feel awkward. He suddenly becomes extremely self-conscious and anxious to get the situation back to normal as quickly as possible.

You can use these facts of applied psychology to control and quiet down the other person's angry emotions. When you find yourself in a tense situation that threatens to get completely out of hand, deliberately lower your voice and keep it down. This, in turn, motivates the other person to lower his voice. As long as he speaks softly, too, he cannot remain angry and high-strung for very long.

Fifteen ways to keep your friendships warm and cordial

It takes a lot of effort to keep your friendships warm and cordial. Neglect them and they'll die from lack of care. Use this 15 point checklist to keep your friendships alive.

1. Always maintain a warm and friendly attitude toward others.
2. Go out of your way to perform some unexpected service for your friends.
3. Compliment another person and praise him for something that he has done.
4. Always keep your word. Never make a promise you cannot keep or a decision you cannot support.
5. Treat your associates at work as close friends of long standing, not just casual acquaintances.
6. Establish a reputation as a reliable person who can be depended on so your friends can always trust you.
7. Go to work with a smile on your face, leaving your personal problems and troubles at home.
8. Never use your position for personal gain at someone else's expense.
9. Don't play favorites; treat every one equally.
10. Have respect for every person's dignity. Treat every woman like a lady and every man like a gentleman.
11. Be sincere in your relationships with others. Don't be a phony. Really mean what you say and say what you mean.
12. Practice the Golden Rule with everyone, especially the daily associates with whom you work.
13. Have a strong belief in the rights of others.
14. Have an abiding interest in the other person's welfare.
15. Be willing to deal with every person as courteously and considerately as if he were your blood relative.

If you will practice consciously the techniques you have learned in this chapter with both your family and your friends so that they are programmed deeply into your subconscious mind and become an integral part of you, I can assure you that your life will be filled with joy and happiness and every day will be worthwhile living.

Although this chapter was written primarily to show you how to use the mighty powers of your subconscious mind to establish good relationships with people outside your home and your family, many of the techniques I have discussed are applicable to both. That is why I have also included specific examples of how to improve your relationships with your wife or husband and your children.

In the next chapter, I will give you even more techniques and methods you can use to improve your family relationships even further.

How You Can Use the Mighty Power of Your Subconscious Mind to Improve Your Family Relationships

13

In the last chapter, I said that husbands and wives who were friends as well as lovers always had the happiest marriages. I also showed you how you could use praise to win your spouse's friendship. And I said that one of the best ways to have a harmonious family relationship was to pay rapt attention to your husband or your wife, and, also, to your children.

In this chapter, I will not only amplify and expand that previous information, but I will also give you some additional powerful methods that you can use to program your subconscious mind so you can make your marriage and your home life much happier.

Just as I have mentioned previously, unless you give your subconscious mind a specific goal to shoot for, it will not work for you. Your goal here is to establish a more harmonious and happy relationship with your entire family. You can achieve that goal you give your subconscious mind when you use the specific techniques that I'll give you in this chapter. When you follow them faithfully,

YOU'LL GAIN THESE SIX MARVELOUS BENEFITS

1. There will be a peaceful and pleasant, happy and joyful atmosphere in your home.

2. A spirit of cheerful cooperation and helpfulness will be evident in every member of your family.

3. There'll be a willingness on everyone's part to work together to solve common family problems.

4. You'll be loved and respected by each member of your family.

5. Your spouse and your children will look to you for guidance and direction.

6. Arguments and disagreements will be virtually nonexistent in your home.

Techniques You Can Use to Gain These Benefits

How to create a happy family atmosphere

Each and every one of us possesses a power we often fail to use properly. *That power is the freedom of choice.* Many people choose to be poor when they need only choose to be rich. Some choose failure instead of success because it is easier. Others choose to be afraid of life when all they need do is step out with courage and take what is rightfully theirs.

What you choose to do about your family life is exactly the same. You have the power to choose the kind of atmosphere that you want in your home. You can choose one that is fun: one that is filled with excitement, joy, and happiness. Or you can choose a home life that is constantly filled with anger and resentment, arguments, and bickering. It's entirely up to you. Let me give you an example of how well this technique will work when it is properly used.

I had an uncle whom I admired greatly, Arthur Harper. He and my aunt Olive were married for more than 50 years before he died. They were always wonderfully happy together. I never once heard a harsh word from either of them for the other, nor did I ever see even an angry glance exchanged between them.

Just before I was married, Uncle Arthur asked me to drop by his house for a chat. "Will you accept a small bit of advice from your old uncle?" he asked. When I said I'd be more than happy to, here's what he told me:

"You can be happy in your marriage if you just choose to be," he said. "That's what your aunt Olive and I did when we were first married. We chose to be happy. If you want your marriage to be successful, I recommend that you do the same. Just choose to be happy. It's really just that simple when you don't complicate it."

If you make that same choice, then you will automatically program your subconscious mind to say kind and courteous, happy and cheerful things to the members of your family. You just cannot choose to be happy and than growl and bark at your family or argue and disagree with them. The two emotions are completely incompatible.

Remember the rule that if you want to get, you must first give. If you use courtesy and tender loving care in your family relationships, that is what you will receive in return. You cannot expect to give nothing to your family and get something back just because it's your family. It won't work. You must make the first move yourself.

All you need do is choose to have a happy home life and the right words will come to you. You won't have to agonize over what to say or how to say it.

Even if you've been married a long time and things don't seem to be going too well, it's never too late to make the decision to be happy with your spouse. When you choose to be happy with your conscious mind, you program your subconscious mind properly so that kindness and courtesy will flow from you with every word you speak. No matter how bad things might seem to be at times, they will always get better when you make that one simple decision: *Choose to be happy*.

How to get up on the right side of the bed

Although it might be a cliché and sound old-fashioned to you, getting up on the right side of the bed in the morning is still an extremely wise procedure. So get in the habit of starting the day off right. Again, it is simply a matter of choice. You can be happy or miserable, whichever you decide to be.

How to do it? Simple. There's another old saying you can use that will help. Instead of saying to yourself, "Good God, it's morning!" just say, "Good morning, God," and go on from there. Greet your wife or husband with a cheerful "Good morning, dear. You must have rested well. You look beautiful (or handsome) this morning."

I don't care whether the sun is shining or whether it's snowing or raining, it can be a terrific day if you will just choose to make it so. Life can be a lot more enjoyable for both you and your family if you start the day off pleasantly with a kind word and a smile instead of a growl and a frown.

Tell yourself that today is going to be the best day of your life and it will be. Yesterday is gone, tomorrow isn't here, so concentrate on making today an outstanding one. Use that attitude and you can infect your family, too.

A former business associate of mine always came to the office with a big smile and a cheerful "Good morning" for everybody.

"What's your secret, Hank?" I once asked him. "How do you manage to be so happy at nine in the morning. Most people don't feel that good until it's quitting time."

"Oh, that's easy, Jim," he said. "My wife wakes me every morning by putting her hand gently on my head and saying, 'It's time to get up, dear. It's a beautiful morning. Your coffee is ready and the morning paper is on the dining room table. I love you.' How could I help but feel good with a greeting like that every morning?"

Something tells me that Hank's wife is one real smart woman. She knows the secret of a happy and successful marriage.

How to get in the habit of saying the cheerful, pleasant thing

It is especially important to develop the habit of cheerful and pleasant conversation when the family is all together if you want to have friendly and harmonious relationships in the home. So always be pleasant to your family no matter how rotten you might feel inside. There's no point in making them miserable just because you're down in the dumps for one reason or another.

It is particularly important to develop the habit of pleasant and cheerful conversation when the family is together. This is especially true at mealtimes. Do not upset everyone's digestion—including your own—by making the family meal a recitation of troubles, anxieties, fears, warnings, and accusations. Make every meal a joyful and happy festive occasion. *Discipline and dinner do not go together.*

Our next door neighbors have two small grandsons who visit them every summer for several weeks. One day the younger one, a seven-year-old, struck up a conversation with me.

"How do you like staying with your grandpa and your grandma?" I asked him.

"I like it fine," he said. "Boy, my grandpa and grandma sure get along real good. They're always saying nice things to each other. They say nice things to me and to my brother, too. They never fight or get mad at each other or at us like my dad and mom do."

Children are especially aware of the kind of family atmosphere they are raised in, no matter how young they are. It's a known fact that abused children grow up to become child abusers themselves. And children with mean and grouchy parents will grow up to be mean and grouchy themselves. So if you want your children to grow up and be the kind of adults whose company other people will enjoy, then raise them in a cheerful and pleasant family atmosphere.

A technique that will work magic in your marriage for you

One of the real secrets to complete joy and happiness in your home is *accepting your partner exactly as he or she is*. Don't try to change your spouse and make him or her over into a second edition of yourself. Don't nag or criticize. You'll never change a person that way. You'll never get a person to do what you want him to do with criticism.

Take your own husband, for example. Have you ever been able to change him very much through all your years of marriage by nagging and finding fault with him? I know you probably thought you had good intentions. You felt you could make him overnight into the kind of person you thought he ought to be, but did you ever really succeed? I doubt it. I know my own wife never did.

Or if you are thinking of making your wife over to fit your own specifications by using criticism, forget it. I failed at that, too. I haven't been able to change her one little bit through all these 45 and more years. She's still the same woman I married. But thank God I failed in all my attempts. I know now that I couldn't have improved on her at all.

Here, now, is a most valuable point for you to remember if you will. *The only person you can ever really change in your life is you, yourself, and you alone—no one else*. So accept your partner just as he or she is. You will never be able to achieve total joy and happiness in your marriage until you do.

How to work this technique if you are newly married

When a couple is first married, they are completely blind to each other's faults. They are too much in love to notice the other person's bad habits. But after the honeymoon is over and they realize some adjustments must be made, there can be a tendency to find fault and criticize each other. Then love can go out the window if they are both not careful.

But this doesn't have to happen. Let me give you some methods you can use to get what you want in your marriage without destroying your happy and loving relationship.

SITUATION: Husband is always leaving the cap off the toothpaste tube.

WRONG: For God's sake, when will you learn to put the cap back on the toothpaste tube anyway? I'm sick and tired of trying to get the toothpaste out when it's all dried up!

RIGHT: Darling, would you mind putting the cap back on the toothpaste tube when you finish? I'd sure appreciate it. Thanks a lot for being so thoughtful.

SITUATION: Wife hangs her stockings over the shower rod to dry and leaves her cosmetics scattered all over the bathroom counter.

WRONG: Why the devil do you always hang your stockings on the shower rod? Can't you find somewhere else to dry them? I can't even take a shower when they're always in my way. And I need a broom to clean up your mess on the bathroom counter. I've never seen so much junk. I can't even find a clean place to shave and wash up.

RIGHT: Honey, I'd appreciate it if you didn't hang your stockings over the shower rod until after I take my shower. I don't like to get them wet or make you wash them all over again. And I wonder if you could pick up the bathroom counter when you're through putting on your makeup. I don't want to spill any soap or water or shaving cream on your things while I'm cleaning up. Thanks so much. Love you for it.

SITUATION: Husband throws his dirty clothes in a corner, tosses his pants on a chair, and drops his shoes where he comes in the door.

WRONG: I'd swear your mother raised a pig instead of a son. If you think I'm going to follow you around picking up after you, you're crazy. I'm sick and tired of your filthy, lazy habits.

RIGHT: Honey, I'd appreciate it if you'd put your dirty things in the clothes hamper and hang your trousers up so they won't get so wrinkled. And this morning I nearly fell over your shoes in the hallway when I was getting ready to go to work. Darling, I can't hold down a job and keep a clean house, too, unless you help me. Would you please do that? Thanks so much for your cooperation, dear. I surely do appreciate it.

I could go on and on with examples like these, but these three should be enough to show you how to solve those small, irritating problems with courtesy and kindness instead of nagging and criticism. Do that, and you'll be able to keep the fires of love and romance burning all your life.

How to have a family love feast

A technique you can use to help establish pleasant and cordial relationships in your home and make your marriage and your home life much happier is to hold a family love feast. Only two basic rules apply: One, no criticism is allowed. Two, only compliments are to be handed out. Here's how to do it.

Gather your entire family in a comfortable setting such as the family room, the den, or the living room. Soft, pleasant background music is permissible, but only if it's turned down real low. However, no television and other interruptions are allowed. Each person takes turns being the subject while all the others tell him the good points they see and like about him. Let me give you some examples:

"I love your awareness of natural beauty. You call my attention sometimes to a beautiful sunset or a gorgeous full moon and I think that's terrific for we can watch it and enjoy it together."

"I want to thank you for picking a hibiscus flower and putting it on the table for me each morning. I do appreciate your loving thoughtfulness."

"I appreciate the way you always put the cap back on the toothpaste tube so it won't dry out."

"You're a warm, loving, and compassionate person, and I love you for that."

"Your smile and a cheerful 'Good morning' get me off to a good start each day. Thanks a lot."

"You really look fantastic in blue (or red or green)."

"I love to hear you sing. You have such a beautiful voice."

"You really have a way with words. You explain everything so clearly I can understand it easily."

"You hit the ball better than anybody I know."

"You're an outstanding speller. I wish I had your talent for that."

"I really do love the cutting board you made for me in your shop class. Thanks a million."

There's absolutely no end to the good things you can say to each other in a family love feast. And it helps the entire family to get along better, to understand each other, and to look for the good qualities instead of the character defects in people.

You can use the same techniques with your friends and associates as well as with your family even if you don't have a "formal" love feast as such. Praise and kind words of love and appreciation for others can make irritable people become warm and outgoing. Sad and despondent persons can become confident and enthusiastic when they are treated to a love feast such as this. So before you dismiss this technique as so much syrupy mush, give it a whirl. When you do, you'll quickly change your mind. You'll find that it's a magic method that makes darned good sense.

How to guide, direct, and control your children without effort

To guide, direct, and control your children without effort so they will always do what you know is best for them to do, *make them happy.* When they are happy, they'll be only too glad to do as you desire.

How do you make a child happy? It takes a lot more than money and material possessions. You can start off by telling your child that you love him and then proving that you do by giving him your full and undivided attention. This is something every child usually needs the most and yet gets the least of: *attention.* As a result, children often feel left out. Lack of attention makes them feel unwanted. You can give them a real sense of being wanted and fulfill their deep need for emotional security by giving them your wholehearted attention.

Praise is the best way to give a person your full attention

Children respond to praise just as much as adults do. If you want your son or daughter to get better grades in school, then praise them for their efforts. When you do that, you are programming their subconscious minds for successful achievement. If you criticize them for their poor grades, those low grades will go even lower for you are then programming their subconscious minds with negative ideas and failure concepts.

I do know that sometimes you must discipline your children. After all, I raised three of my own. But good discipline does not include criticism. Discipline should be reasonable and firm, yet kind and friendly. Parents in unhappy families don't realize this, but in a happy family there is seldom any reason for discipline. People usually discipline themselves in happy families.

So give your children a happy, pleasant atmosphere, encourage their efforts with kind words of praise, work with them, play with them, make them feel they belong by letting them take part in family projects, and you'll find that the necessity for discipline seldom exists.

Your children will do what you ask them to do. When discipline is handled in this way, you can enjoy your children, just as Mike Turner does.

"One summer a few years ago when Warren was 16, he and I went on a month-long trip throughout the west in a camper, just the two of us," Mike told me. "We did everything together just as two buddies would. We took turns driving the pickup, cooking the meals, washing the dishes, making the beds. Not once during the trip did I tell him what to do. I treated him as an equal.

"After we were back home, Warren paid me a compliment I will always remember. 'Dad, this has been the best time of my life,' he said. 'I'll always remember this trip for I've learned from it that you are my friend as well as my father.'"

I know you must give guidance and counsel to your children, but if you really want to enjoy them and make your home life much happier, drop that parent role as often as you can so you can be a friend as well as a father or a mother. This approach will bring you a wonderful new relationship with them.

How a wife can help her husband become highly successful

A wife can help her husband become highly successful by the simple act of using words of praise for what he does. As I have said, praise is the best way in the world to program another person's subconscious mind positively. So if you want your husband to get ahead and be successful in his work, then don't criticize him for not bringing home a bigger paycheck. Instead, praise him for his hard work and for all he does for you. Praise builds his self-confidence and helps him get ahead. Let me show you how important that can be to both of you.

Charles H., president of a large company employing several thousand people, told me that big business and corporations want to find out more about the wife before a man is promoted to a top-level of responsibility.

"I, myself, am more interested in whether a wife can give her husband a feeling of confidence in himself than I am in her good looks or social acceptability," Charles says.

"You see, if she gives her husband the feeling that she is pleased with him and with his work, and if she praises him in every way possible, it's about like getting a shot of adrenalin every time he comes home.

"His wife's praise sends him off each morning filled with the self-confidence that he can solve any problem that comes along. That's the kind of person we need in our top executive positions. That kind of wife can help put him there."

How to make your spouse the most important person in your life

Of the 14 basic needs and desires we all have, the desire to be important is the most dominant one of all in nearly everyone. So make your mate the most important person in your life by what you say and by what you do and you will never fail. Here are three specific ways you can do exactly that:

1. *Think that your mate is the most important person* in the whole wide world. The first rule to use is simply to convince yourself that your spouse is the most important person in your life. Do this, and you won't have to pretend. Your attitude will come across to him or to her loud and clear without even trying.

Not only that, you won't have to use any phony gimmicks or artificial tricks to make this technique work. Your relations with your mate will be on an honest and sincere basis as they should be. As you think, so shall you believe, and as you believe, so shall it be. Act as if it were true and it will be true.

2. *Pay close attention to everything she or he says and does*. The most common complaint of wives is this: "He never notices me . . . never pays any attention to me or to what I say . . . takes me for granted . . . treats me like an old shoe . . . "

Does your wife have a new hairdo? Tell her how beautiful it makes her look. Is she wearing a new dress? Compliment her on her good taste. Thank her for the wonderful dinner she prepared for you. The same sort of advice works for the wife, too.

3. *Always praise . . . never criticize*. You've heard me mention this several times before, but it is such a valuable technique I could never discuss it too often. Praise is the most powerful tool you can use to feed a person's ego, make him feel important, not only to you, but also to himself, and program his subconscious mind for successful achievement.

Criticism, on the other hand, destroys. Criticism destroys people. It creates enemies. It ruins friendships. It destroys love and marriages. In fact, I cannot think of one single thing criticism does that is of any value whatever to anyone.

So if you want a harmonious and friendly relationship with your spouse, never criticize. Praise instead. Praise creates energy. It makes a person work harder, more effectively, and with greater enthusiasm, because praise makes the person feel proud of himself and what he has done.

Simply say to your spouse, "I am so proud of you." These are magic words, for he or she will do whatever you want when you use them. You just can't miss when you praise a person for what he has done.

And now on to the last chapter: *How You Can Use Perseverance to Achieve Total Success*.

How You Can Use Perseverance to Achieve Total Success

14

PERSEVERANCE: THE KEY TO SUCCESS

I have now given you all the information you need to program your subconscious mind for success in everything you do. I've shown you how you can use it to attain your innermost desires: the love and respect of your spouse and your children, your friends and neighbors, your business associates. You've also seen how you can use the mighty powers of your subconscious mind to gain your desires of fame, fortune, power, and how to stay healthy . . . as well as how to rid yourself of fear, anxiety, and worry forever, and how to get rid of such undesirable habits as excessive drinking, smoking, procrastination, and a bad temper.

The only thing that could prevent your success now is a lack of perseverance, so that is what this final chapter is all about. Although it is a shorter chapter than the others, its importance is not diminished by its brevity.

How You Can Make Perseverance Pay Off for You

Of all the personal character traits you will need to develop to succeed in life, perseverance is without a doubt one of the most important, if not the most important. Without perseverance, nothing really worthwhile can ever be accomplished. It is the one major success factor that quickly separates the doers from the wishers.

It is ever so easy to be full of fire, enthusiasm, and persistence about doing a difficult job or working on a complex project as long as everything is going all right. But it's a tough proposition to handle when it starts raining inside. That's when the wishers quit and the doers keep right on doing.

But you can always use temporary setbacks to help you on your way to successful achievement of your goals if you refuse to give up or acknowledge defeat. Read the biographies of great people, and you will find, almost without exception, that each one of them was down for the count more than once, but they always bounced back. It is usually not possible to win total success without paying a high price of some sort, often in the form of opposition, hardship, and setbacks of one kind or the other. Few are those who can cross the river of life without getting their feet wet.

Without perseverance, there is little hope for success. Perseverance means to hold out, to last to the end, to remain steadfast and loyal. Perseverance is the ability to put up with pain, pressure, fatigue, distress, and disappointment. It is the golden key that can turn temporary failure into permanent success, defeat into victory. Those who make it to the top have one character trait in common: perseverance. As I once heard it put, "Perseverance is when your hands and feet keep on working even though your head says it can't be done."

One of our presidents described perseverance this way: "Nothing in the world can take the place of persistence. Talent will not; nothing is more common than unsuccessful men with talent. Genius will not; unrewarded genius is almost a proverb. Education alone will not; the world is full of educated derelicts. Persistence and determination are omnipotent. The slogan 'Press on!' has solved and always will solve the problems of the human race."

That is the kind of perseverance you will need to achieve total success. Nothing else will ever do.

How You Can Use Repetition to Achieve Success

Memory experts say that if you want to memorize something simple, like a short poem, for instance, it takes approximately 42 repeti-

tions to make a permanent imprint in the memory banks of your subconscious mind. They also say that if you want to learn something long
and difficult, say Lincoln's Gettysburg Address, for example, it will
take nearly 500 repetitions before you can recite it without a mistake or
without hesitation.

Repetition is a powerful factor in effective programing of your
subconscious mind. It serves two main purposes. First of all, the conscious mind cannot act on what it does not understand. Repetition, especially when a proposition is presented in numerous ways, serves to
make the idea clearer.

Second, repetition wears down the resistance of any contrary or
conflicting ideas which are preventing the ready acceptance of the
proposition.

As Job once said in effect, "The water wears down the stones."
That simple statement is one of the clearest pictures of the power of
repetition. Let me give you another example, that of the pile-driver.

Some years ago, I had a deep well dug so I could have a constant
and inexpensive source of water for my lawn. You see, in spite of all its
lakes and being surrounded by water on three sides, Florida never has
enough rainfall. Grass must be watered constantly throughout the year
or lawns will die out and become nothing but barren weed patches.

The gentleman who dug my well brought a pile-driving machine
to my yard. It had a heavy iron weight about three inches wide and
several feet long. This weight was suspended on a chain and was pulled
high up into the air. Then it was dropped straight down to make a
small indentation each time it struck the ground. This process went on
for three days until the hole was deep enough to use a drill to go
through hard rock and limestone. Finally the hole was hundreds of
feet deep. It was then lined with an iron pipe and when the drill finally
reached the aquifer, water spouted up several feet high into the air.

This cumulative process, the constant hammering, the continuous
driving force of the pile-driver, eventually overcame the resistance of
earth, rock, and limestone to give me a deep well with a reliable source
of cold, clear, fresh water to use on my lawn.

This is the same sort of repetition that causes men of obscurity to
become famous and well-known. It is this singleness of purpose that
lifts a person out of the depths of poverty to the heights of prosperity.
This same repetition allows your subconscious mind to reach the goals
you have given it, no matter what they are, so you, too, can become
successful.

Why Practice Makes for Perfection

This same repetition is required, not only to memorize something and to program it deep into the memory banks of the subconscious mind, but also to perfect one's natural talents and abilities.

A famous concert violinist applied this principle of repetition to his musical talents. He maintained a rigorous eight-hour-daily practice schedule throughout his entire career. Asked why he persisted in practicing even after he had become world-renowned for his musical excellence, he said, "If I neglect to practice for a month, my audience knows the difference. If I neglect it for a week, my wife notices the difference. But if I do not practice even for one single day, then I can tell the difference!"

Another gentleman, a world-famous concert pianist, not only physically practices at the piano, but he also practices continually in his mind even when he is away from the piano. A recognized authority on teaching the piano highly recommends this procedure. A new composition should be first gone over in the mind, he says. It should be memorized and played in the mind before ever touching the fingers to the keyboard.

One of the best known golf instructors in the world teaches people to picture in their minds exactly what they are going to do on the golf course before they ever pick up a club. He says that golf is 90 percent mental, eight percent physical, and two percent mechanical.

If you are a weekend golfer, as I am, and you want to improve your score, you can if you will first picture in your mind exactly what it is you want to do. Picture the end result—that is to say, see the ball going where you want it to go—and your subconscious mind will take over and direct your muscles. Even if your grip is wrong, and your stance is not the best, your subconscious mind will still take care of that by directing your muscles to do whatever is necessary to compensate for your errors in form.

This is not theory. It is a fact. By following this procedure, I've been able to break 90 for the first time with no actual practice whatsoever. Others who have tried this method have been able to chop as much as eight or ten strokes off their scores.

How You Can Make Perseverance One of Your Best Habits

Most people think of a habit as being something bad, but that is not true. My dictionary defines a habit as being a tendency to act in a certain way, or to do a certain thing a certain way at all times. So a habit can be good, like brushing your teeth regularly, always being on time, that sort of thing.

A bad habit can be changed by converting it into a good one, simply by repetition and perseverance. For instance, a friend of mine, I'll just call him Al, used to have a severe drinking problem. It was so bad that he finally turned to Alcoholics Anonymous for help. He has not had a drink for more than five years now.

When I asked Al how he was able to solve his drinking problem, he said, "By persevering. Actually, it was very easy once I understood the nature of my problem. A.A. taught me that I wasn't an alcoholic because I drank too much. Instead, I drank too much because I was an alcoholic. I realized that my drinking was simply a bad habit, so I changed habits. I got into the habit of *not* drinking. I continued that habit of not drinking and I succeeded in staying sober by persistence and perseverance."

You can do the same. You can change your bad habit, whatever it is, into a good one—and if you persevere, you, too, will succeed, just as Al did.

Successful Achievement Always Requires Perseverance

The most successful salespeople never give up. Statistics show that 80 percent of all sales are made on the fifth call, yet 48 percent of salesmen never go back after the first unsuccessful call. Twenty-five percent quit after the second call, 12 percent give it up after the third one, and five percent throw in the towel after the fourth time. But ten percent of the salesmen keep calling and they make 80 percent of the sales.

As you can quickly see from this, persistence pays off. Another friend of mine is a top-notch life insurance salesman. I know he is persistent because in spite of my never buying any insurance from him, he still kept coming back. One day I said, "Frank, how many times are you going to call on me before you give up trying to sell me insurance?"

"It depends upon which one of us dies first!" he said. Now that's what I call perseverance.

Upon hearing what Frank said, I finally gave up and bought a policy from him.

"Why did you finally change your mind, Jim?" he asked.

"To tell you the truth, Frank, I couldn't fight you off any longer," I replied. "Your perseverance paralyzed my resistance."

You cannot keep a persistent man down for long. I know you've seen the TV commercials plugging Birdseye frozen vegetables. But you probably don't know that in the beginning, Clarence E. Birdseye lost all his money—everything he had, even the money he had borrowed on his life insurance—when his frozen food business failed.

But that didn't stop Clarence Birdseye. He persevered because he still believed that there was a market in frozen foods. He started over, borrowing a corner of a friends's ice plant for his experiments. Did he succeed? Well, he later sold out his frozen food company for $22,000,000! In spite of his original failure, he succeeded because of his perseverance and his belief in what he was doing.

Stubbornness and Perseverance Are Not the Same

You must differentiate between perseverance and mule-headed stubbornness if you want to succeed. The stubborn man refuses to give up, but he never changes his methods. He refuses to admit he is wrong and continually beats his head against a wall. Even though he is not getting the results he wants, he refuses to admit his mistakes and try a new approach.

Whenever you have a setback or a temporary failure, you can persevere and succeed if you will use these three simple steps:

1. *Convince yourself that there has to be a way* to do what you want. Remember that a problem is insoluble only when you believe it can't be solved. When you believe that solutions are possible, you will eventually attract the right one to you.

2. *Back off and start fresh.* Many times you're so close to the problem you can't see the solution. Take a breather and then come back for another go at it.

3. *Be persistent; never give up.* The history books are full of examples of people who succeeded even after failure because they never gave up. Lincoln, Edison, even Nixon, though he had to resign from the Presidency in disgrace, were persistent and eventually reached their goals because of their persistence.

You can reach all your goals, too. All you need do is program what you want into your subconscious mind, persevere, and everything you desire can be yours.

Index